The
Challenging
Child
Toolbox

75 Mindfulness-Based Practices, Tools and Tips for Therapists

Mitch Abblett, PhD

The Challenging Child Toolbox © copyright 2018 by Mitch Abblett.

Published by:
PESI Publishing & Media
PESI, Inc.
3839 White Ave.
Eau Claire, WI 54703

Cover Design: Amy Rubenzer
Editing By: Bookmasters
Layout: Amy Rubenzer & Mayfly Designs

Printed in the United States of America
ISBN: 9781683731702

PESI
Publishing
& Media
www.publishing.pesi.com

Contents

Chapter 3:
Emphasizing the Validity of Children's Inner Experience . . . 51

Chapter 4:
Foundational Skills of Clinical Presence 71

Chapter 8:
Using and Teaching a Proactive Mindset 153

Chapter 9:
Finding and Fueling Purpose
for You and Your Clients 175

Chapter 10:
Focusing on Process vs. Outcome in Work with EBD
Child and Teen Clients 193

Introduction

Welcome to *The Challenging Child Toolbox*! You ended up here because you're likely looking for some principles, pointers, and practices that will help you in your clinical interventions with child clients whose emotions and behaviors can be a "tad" challenging to work with. Don't worry if you've been at a complete loss for how to help some of these young clients at one point or another: So have I, and I write books about this sort of work! If you've been frustrated, worried, saddened, doubtful, confused, and downright angry from time to time in working with these kids, you're in good company, and you're in the right place. I hope this book becomes a handy go-to resource that helps you get out of the ditches that are inevitable and get treatment back on track with these young people.

Let's pause for a moment before we get started and consider the following clinical situation:

My 12-year-old client Sam's tantrum that day had the feel of the cartoon character the Tasmanian Devil as he whirled through my office. "I wanna call my mom now!" he yelled. I'd told him that making a call at that moment was not an option—that he needed to calm down first so we could solve whatever nuance of unmet expectation or perceived social slight was afflicting him.

Sam lunged for my desk and the phone sitting atop it, beginning to dial frantically. My embarrassment-prone mind was thankful I was alone in the group practice that evening. I had no colleagues to witness my incompetent management of my bipolar disorder- and PTSD-diagnosed boy client. "Come on, buddy," I said. "Let's talk this out. There's no need—"

"Shut up, A$&^%$!" he yelled. I stepped forward and puffed myself up in an attempt to create a human bubble around him—a bubble that seemed about to pop at any second. I said that he was making the person who cared for him very nervous. Why I felt the urge to speak of myself in the third person was almost as notable as my desperate offer to give him some of my sandwich if he'd please simply calm down. "F&%& you!" he screamed. "I'm calling her now!"

And then I did it—I impulsively reached and unplugged the phone jack from the wall behind my desk. Sam's fury ignited into desk shoving and flinging a chair. I called 911 from an adjoining office and, after a stand-off there in my office during which he kept the paramedics at bay with a sharp and threateningly wielded pencil, they took him to be screened for admission to a psychiatric inpatient unit.

Sam lay on the gurney inside the ambulance the entire short ride to the hospital. In stark contrast to his swearing and yelling during his tantrum in my office, he lay like a discarded mannequin on the gurney. The paramedic who sat with us in the back tried to get Sam to answer a few simple questions during the ride: "What's your birthday?" "What seems to be the problem today?" "What medication do you take?" but he did not respond.

I looked away and out the back window. I wanted to watch anything but this boy's face. It was reddened and tight from the unfortunately synergistic mix of sadness, fear, and anger squatting behind it. I'm not sure if I remember accurately whether Sam's eyes were welling with tears during the ride to the hospital. It may very well have been my own clamped-off crying my memory pasted onto his face. I do remember how he wouldn't look at me as we rode to the hospital, the adrenaline-strangled silence inside the ambulance in stark contrast to the siren's wail. The only question he responded to was, "What seems to be the problem today?"

"Ask him," he said flat and raw as a cancer diagnosis. "*He* called you." Sam had indeed crossed a threshold, and he certainly needed to go to the hospital. He trashed my office and made me feel as trapped and powerless as he did. Sam had known far too much failure, upheaval, and loss in his 12 years. I felt I had far too few years of experience to know how to best help him.

Sound at all familiar? Perhaps with less (or more intensity) than this particular episode, you wouldn't have picked up this book if episodes like (or leaning toward) this were not either in the past or forecast for the future of your clinical practice.

Why You Need The Challenging Child Toolbox

Across the years of my professional work in residential, inpatient, outpatient, and therapeutic day school programs, I have stubbed my toes enough in working with youth who struggle to manage their intense emotions and behavior to have learned a few things that might benefit clinicians facing the challenge of this work. The bottom line across approaches to treatment is to ground these children in consistency and predictability of supportive and yet direct, accountability-enhancing intervention. It's crucial to provide this foundation in order to create a healing context of safety, as well as to slowly take the charge out of their learned patterns through skills training in understanding and modulating their emotions and behavior. It's also important to help kids write a new narrative—a new inner story—of themselves, as opposed to whatever scripts were laid down across the course of their developmental history.

Why is it so difficult to work effectively with children who both externalize (e.g., swearing, threatening, hitting, kicking, destroying or throwing things) and internalize (e.g., extreme school avoidance, emotional numbing, panic attacks) or those kids who exhibit behaviors in both symptomatic camps? How do you even begin to intervene effectively with these kids, and how do you get on top of the inevitable reactivity you experience from trying to help them? These are the questions this book addresses, and herein you will find concrete tools for getting traction in your work and (dare I say!) even enjoying the process and arriving at a sense of self-efficacy along the way.

A central theme you will encounter throughout *The Challenging Child Toolbox* is that children who struggle to manage their emotions and behavior are reacting in an understandable, though maladaptive, way. Their nervous systems responded to the demands of their life circumstances by (after many learning situations with others) developing emotional and behavioral patterns in order to minimize pain and discomfort for themselves. Although the swearing, hitting, or shutting down might have helped them feel better or avoid certain negative experiences in the short run, the problem is that in the long run, it got them stuck in a destructive cycle.

You, the professional caregiver, are not the cause of their problems, and (as you'll hear me suggest throughout the book) neither are these kids! They need help in learning to hang out with discomfort without lashing out (or pulling into themselves) and need you—the helper—to provide the conditions for learning these more skillful means.

The Contents of Your Toolbox

The goal of *The Challenging Child Toolbox* is to give you specific principles, pointers, and practices to enhance your interventions with **emotionally and behaviorally-challenged children**. This book is NOT, however, a comprehensive treatment manual with all the evidence-based intervention techniques for effective intervention with this population of clients.

The Challenging Child Toolbox targets the weak links in the standard treatment protocols— the vulnerable spots that tend to hover in and around the therapeutic relationship as well as the HOW of intervention (as opposed to the WHAT of a specific technique).

It is for this reason that the toolbox is divided into three primary sets of tools:

- **Principles** . . . These are the 10 core themes to strike in your interventions and in the therapeutic relationship itself with child clients who struggle to manage emotions and behavior. These principles are meant to organize and galvanize your perspective on this population, yourself, and the work in a way that helps you develop sure footing for your day-to-day work. They are the beacons to guide you when things seem off-track or absolutely derailed. Principles are not scripts or recipes to be rigidly implemented; they are to be aligned to, resonated with. Multiple methods can be used to effectively demonstrate these principles. The evidence that you're on track with a given principle for working with child and teen clients will be insight and "feel" of effectiveness in your own experience as you embody them. Your clients will feel and benefit from this synergy between action and governing principles as well.

- **Pointers** . . . Here, we have specific interventions that, in addition to other cognitive-behavioral, behavior analytic, and mindfulness-based techniques, can be helpful in solidifying child client engagement in these techniques and methods. They are a form of "psychic glue" holding both them AND you in the treatment, healing, and skill development process. They also have been shown (through much trial and error with many child clients of my own—and for those I've supervised) to enhance and at times repair therapeutic relationships. Pointers are nuts and bolts things you can *do* during clinical interactions.

- **Practices** . . . There is a growing literature supporting that the practice of self-compassion leads to significant reductions in stress, burnout, and the negative effects of anxiety and depression (Neff & McGehee, 2010; MacBeth & Gumley, 2012). Working regularly with children struggling with **emotional and behavioral disorders (EBD, for short, for the remainder of the book)** can certainly lead you toward more than your fair share of these undesirable outcomes. Crucial in this toolbox are mindfulness-related practices designed to be brief, accessible methods for cutting your stress, managing countertransference, and even cultivating meaning and enjoyment working with challenging kids.

So again, the toolbox is not a one-stop shopping resource for all things EBD intervention. It is, however, a very important set of tools that fill some holes in the treatment literature. The WHAT of effective intervention (e.g., cognitive-behavioral techniques) will fall flat for clinicians who struggle to manage the HOW of their interventions (e.g., timing, tone, relational messaging, perspective or philosophy of behavior). And for those of you at all familiar with the psychotherapy research literature, the relational aspect of psychotherapy has been consistently shown to be the best predictor of treatment outcomes (Flückiger et al., 2011). More than theoretical orientation, specific technical focus, and demographic variables of clinician and client, the quality of the therapeutic relationship (or "alliance," as it's typically referred to in the literature) carries the day (and the variance of the research data). Clinicians working with children presenting with (EBD) Emotional Behavior Disorder stand much better odds at reaching positive outcomes with resources such as those included in *The Challenging Child Toolbox*, which will help you build the sound therapeutic context serving as a foundation for children's healing and positive change.

Children with EBD have suffered varying levels of derailment of their emotional, social, and cognitive development. Therefore, they need professionals to give extra attention to creating a supportive, structured, and empowering treatment context. If you are not exceedingly proactive with your interventions, you end up like me in the earlier example—chasing your own knee-jerk reactions instead of shaping responses that coach and lead kids toward more adaptive functioning. Here are some of the skill sets *The Challenging Child Toolbox* will help you develop:

- **Conceptualizing emotional and behavioral patterns in children:** It is tempting to get stuck in viewing these children as "intentionally" acting out and being disruptive. Doing so sparks your own negative reactivity and decreases your effectiveness. With the principles, pointers, and practices in this toolbox, you'll learn to cultivate, sustain, and communicate the "big picture" in working with EBD kids and how relationships (such as with you) can become a primary battleground for them as they struggle toward healing.

- **Therapeutic relational development:** A treatment relationship that puts the premium on quality of connection as opposed to compliance will have fewer challenges and obstacles to overcome. Tools in this area will lead the children you work with to feel supported and contained, and you (by the way) will feel more engaged and supported as well. This toolbox will help you learn to go out of your way to note and build up the strengths in these children and nudge them to look to you and others in their lives for support when their strengths are less evident.

- **Prompting in the use of self-regulation strategies:** Without shoving strategies down kids' throats, many tools in this book facilitate children's skills for more adaptive ways of soothing their bodies and channeling their energy. Here, we don't wait for the behavior to erode and, instead, lead the child into an activity that simultaneously engages and teaches. It's common to get "stuck in the headlights" when young clients are escalating. What if you lead them "pied-piper" style into some yoga poses or a sensory strategy? At the very least, you'll burn a few calories!

- **Compassionate limit-setting:** YES, you need to set limits with these children. YES, you must be consistent despite the genesis of their issues. And YES, you must be highly attuned to the child, letting him or her know that you know there are understandable bad feelings behind their not-so-nice actions.

- **Facilitating feedback loops:** The principles, pointers, and practices in this book help you to circle back to the EBD child and to their parents. Don't merely report the facts of an episode, but connect with them. Talk about the emotions and the ripple effects of behaviors. Ask for their experience (and really hear it). Make them feel like crucial links in learning new patterns for the future.

- **Repair work:** Children who act out from a place of reactivity are well aware that they've done so. They may not move on like other clients and, therefore, benefit greatly from extra attention to repairing therapeutic relationship ruptures. This toolbox supports you in helping them repair the damage caused by their extreme behavior. It's a dual message: "I care about you, and I care about your caring about others."

- **Address burnout and vicarious trauma:** If you've worked with enough EBD children, you know a bit about this already. Hopefully, you've learned the crucial importance of addressing your own excessive reactivity—the shutting down, avoidance, numbing, snappishness, and so forth. The bottom line for this toolbox: Don't take others' pain deep into yourself.

How to Use This Toolbox

There are lots of ways you can use this book. You can:

- Go through and read and learn the various tools in order or …

- Pick a tool that's relevant to a current obstacle in your work with a particular child and spend time bringing it to bear.

- You might try picking a specific PRINCIPLE and linked POINTER and PRACTICE and spending a week or more focusing on them before moving to another.

- Pick your favorite or the most helpful PRACTICES throughout the book and use them to manage your own stress or reactivity to the work or to enhance your enjoyment of a particular aspect of your daily work.

- You can pair with a colleague and read through and support each other in using the POINTERS and PRACTICES together, perhaps teaching them to one another.

- The PRINCIPLES can be helpful discussion topics/prompts for clinical courses, supervision sessions, or staff meetings.

- There are lots of options! This is not to be used as a textbook. It truly is meant to be an active, engaging toolbox building the best interventions and treatment contexts for kids who don't always make it a straightforward process!

What's Impossible About This Book

I'll be blunt ... It's impossible to fail or to use this book incorrectly (unless you beat yourself over the head with it in frustration from doing this work!). Although the book is not a step-by-step manual for how to do the best treatment with challenging child clients, if you align with the PRINCIPLES, and spend time giving the various intervention POINTERS and self-management PRACTICES a try, you will certainly improve your ability to work with these at-time daunting-to-work-with kids.

As you explore the various tools in this book, take your time and listen deeply to what they are teaching you—not only about how to do the best work, but why this work is so important. Working with children with emotional and behavioral challenges need not be a burden. For some (and I'd argue those who internalize these tools), it can become something closer to a calling.

As we end this discussion of how to go about doing the best work with this group of clients, let me summarize things with something written from the perspective of the "challenging" child themselves. It is important to wonder about the voices of these children—what would they say about what they most want and need (if they could even begin to more directly do so)? Research and clinical experience are crucial, but so is the experience of those we're intending to care for.

Things I Need You to Know

I need lots of attention.
Even when I swear at you, I still need your attention.
I will talk endlessly about stuff like video games because that's all I'm really good at.
I will do odd, quirky things that always seem to get weird looks from people.
And when I tell you I don't care, it really means I just don't know how to let myself care.
The four letter word that makes me the most uncomfortable is "SPED."

I don't want to be here because it means I failed in order to get here.
I've never belonged to things much in the past.
I learned a long time ago to reject you before you can reject me.
Did I mention that I want your attention?

I'll be looking for ways to get control by hitting your buttons,
And by "splitting" you against one another,
And against my family as well,
And by sparking other kids to get in trouble.
Because control is something I've been without for quite a while.

My file says I'm not retarded but I think I am.
My diagnosis crawls through my file like some sort of bug I want to squash.
You will misunderstand me.
You will assume I'm being "lazy" or "manipulative" or "nasty" on purpose.
I really just don't know what else to do to not have to feel the way I feel.

Every day, my medication is a reminder of how I'm sick but you can't see how.
Bald kids with cancer get cards and warm smiles.
I get blamed and punished because I'm bad.
And even if you tell me I'm not bad, I won't believe you.
It's your job to say nice things to me, so again, I won't believe you.
But did I already say (because it's hard for me to focus on things and I forget) …
I really want your attention?

I just want a chance to fit in; to do something right once in a while.
I just want to feel okay for a day.
I just want my family to be proud of me for once.
I just don't want to have to remember all the bad stuff from before all the time.
I just want you to follow through on your promises to me (because others haven't).
I just don't want you to confuse my actions with who I really want to be in the future.
And yes, before I forget, the future means almost nothing to me.

I will try to embarrass you.
I will try to make you angry.
I will try to make you nervous.
I will try to make you hate me.
Because then I will know I'm not crazy for feeling these things myself.
Because then I will know who I can begin to trust.

And trust is five letters because it's better even though it's hard.
Four letter words are just easy but if I can get to five letters then,
Maybe I can make it to six, and then …
Maybe I can start CARING …
And then maybe, just maybe, I'll let myself believe I deserve your attention.

The Ten Caregiver Commandments

I. NO "BAD" KIDS (OR CAREGIVERS)

II. WE'RE WIRED TO CONNECT AND REACT

III. EQUIVALENCE IN EXPERIENCE

IV. YOUR PRESENCE IS THE GREATEST GIFT

V. AUTHENTICITY IS THE "REAL" SECRET

VI. KIDS NEED "HOLDING ENVIRONMENTS"

VII. IRONCLAD COMMUNICATION (THE 3 C'S)

VIII. THE PROACTIVITY MINDSET

IX. SEEING "BEYOND" BEHAVIOR TO PURPOSE

X. HOLDING OUTCOMES "LIGHTLY"

Chapter 1

Reframing
Children's
Problem
Behavior

No "Bad" Kids (or Therapists)

What (It Is)

As a practicing psychologist, many clients over the years have taught me a great deal about how they were regarded by parents, teachers, and other caregivers when they "misbehaved," "disrupted," or "manipulated" others as kids. They taught me the importance of learning to balance holding children accountable with a heavy dose of compassion.

My clients (some kids and some adults contemplating their upbringing) very much wish more people who were charged with their care had learned how to see and reach "behind" their behavior. Though they may have indeed misbehaved, and though they may acknowledge the need for consequences for these actions, they just want people to understand what was really driving things—an unseen inner landscape of turmoil and stress.

A shift in perspective is needed for clinicians, parents, teachers, and all onlookers of kids who are struggling to manage their emotions and behavior. Studies, such as those by Harvard social psychologist Daniel Gilbert, have repeatedly documented a perceptual distortion called "correspondence bias," which is common to everyone when they make judgments about the source or cause of others' actions.[1] Basically, when looking at others, unless there are clear external or environmental causes that render the person "blameless" (such as a young child with cancer who did nothing to create her situation), we tend to assume (incorrectly) that people's behavior is the inevitable and complete result of their own internal traits (or conscious choices). The person who cuts us off in traffic is undeniably a jerk. My client who wanted to have the school nurse help with the welt on his head was an anxious "manipulator." They *chose* and, therefore, *caused* this behavior to result. It is easy to see then how our empathy gets blocked for such kids.

Why (It Matters)

Kids who are struggling with chronic emotional and behavioral concerns deserve the benefit of compassionate doubt. The adult needs to let go of assumptions and agendas and sincerely wonder aloud to the child about what might be stuck for them and *from the child's own perspective*.

We need to see past the behavior, past the blame, and focus on intent to the fact that kids are looking to do the best they can despite difficult emotional experiences we're not even aware of.

Joe's teacher, and many parents and caregivers, are trying to be compassionate and helpful—even trying to see behind the emotions and behavior of the moment. Although this intent is good, it often falls short because the kid does not sense the compassionate effort that comes from genuine *curiosity* about what's happening for the child.

Children will come to care about and respond to our help when our responses to their behavior clearly send the message of acceptance and caring. Our willingness to make a practice of such perspective-taking gives them the opportunity to connect with us around that inner struggle, get the help they need, and let loose on what they're capable of doing, achieving, and being.

When or Where (It Applies)

Though his research focuses on the interactions of married couples, psychologist John Gottman's concept of "bidding" for connection is relevant to those working with children with EBD.[2] When people shout, nag, cajole, withdraw, accuse, and get downright nasty in their relationships, they are, in true "auction" style, making a "bid" for connection—trying to let the other person know that they have an emotional need that needs attention. All clinicians should realize that children who exhibit disruptive and displacing behaviors are in fact doing the same thing—**using their behavior to signal what needs attention in themselves.**

All behavior is a message, and behind any child's misbehavior is a message that is easy to miss. Not that his behavior does not merit consequences (we'll address this later in this toolbox), but nonetheless it's crucial to wonder what the child is *really* trying to say. It's important to "hurry up and wait" and take a moment or two before heaping on the consequences in a reactive manner to consider what's really driving him to be such a "noodge" at school and/or at home. It requires that adults be willing and able to slow down, catch, and categorize their *own* reactions. Only then can they choose the best interventions to manage tough behavior.

In the following relational compass, all interpersonal behavior can be quickly categorized according to what it "looks like" as well as what the "message" is really about. This figure is a tool for helping caregivers working with EBD children to gain in-the-moment perspective when kids are struggling with their behavior. It's a tool to help see the real message behind behavior, catch one's inner reactivity, and be more likely to respond in helpful ways. The compass asks caregivers to categorize (and it's easier than it might seem at first) the child's behavior by how external (or observable) versus internal (inner experiential) it appears, as well as how attuned/connected to their emotional needs and perspective the child's behavior is. The caregivers (you) can then ask the same of themselves and their behavior, and what they are feeling "pulled" to do in reaction to the child.

The Relational Compass

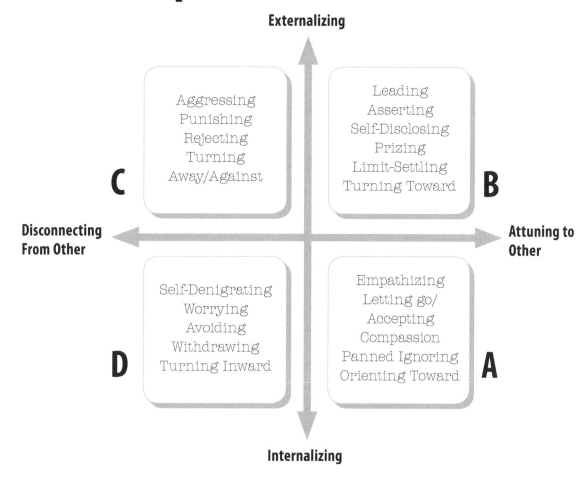

How (To Cultivate It)

In the example from the Introduction to this book, my child client Sam's behavior is external and disconnected from my needs/perspective when he was escalating his behavior and acting out. His behavior clearly falls on the "left" and is likely to disrupt others, as well as his own learning. Understandably, I experienced a reactive "pull" toward the left on the figure, as well—thinking to myself (again, I write and teach this stuff!) that *Sam is doing this again, on purpose* and, therefore, getting anxious and reactive and trying to clamp down on his behavior.

As we'll discuss throughout the tools in this book, it is helpful to build a new mindset for viewing challenging behavior in clients. This new mindset begins with emblazoning the following question into your brain when faced with any maladaptive interpersonal behavior from a child client: *What is the message behind this behavior?* What's driving this child to up the ante in this situation? We'll come back to these questions time and again and not only provide a framework for understanding them, but also how to intervene from them effectively.

Now, let's assume I had shown a more ideally skillful response to Sam and had been able to psychologically step back and catch the "pull" toward reactivity. What might be the ideal "right-sided" interventions for Sam and all other emotionally and behaviorally-challenged youth? This is what you'll find within *The Challenging Child Toolbox.*

The Light at the End of the Tunnel Vision

Get Oriented

When a client is struggling and exhibiting problematic behavior, or even when you're just hearing about it from their parents, it's tempting (and completely normal based on our brain's evolved wiring for emotional reactivity) to jump to conclusions based on well-researched biases in human cognition. Just because you're a clinician does not imbue you with immunity to such influences. You (and I) have the same essential brain structure that prehistoric Homo sapiens had 40,000 years ago. It helped us jump to conclusions that atypical, sudden changes in others' behavior might prove dangerous and, therefore, helped our ancestors to survive. We live in a less physically dangerous world with much more social and emotional nuance, and yet we're walking into our sessions with challenging EBD child clients with our frontal cerebral cortexes tied behind the backside of our limbic systems! These emotionally reactive biases may have helped us survive in the past, but they've facilitated a lot of suffering in the present. They foster a sense of tunnel vision, whereby we snap to judgments (including diagnoses and ineffective interventions) and fail to take in the full truth of a given clinical situation for a child.

Listen (To What Actually IS)

Before launching into a behavioral, cognitive-behavioral, or even a mindfulness-based intervention with a child client, and particularly if that client has been (or is currently) struggling to manage their emotions/behavior, consider whether you may be falling under the influence of a cognitive bias. There are many (see the "References" at the back of the book for a more exhaustive discussion[3]). For the purposes of doing your best work with EBD child clients, here are two of the "heavy hitters" of the various cognitive/perceptual biases:

- **Confirmation bias:** Making a judgment or conclusion about current functioning/events based SOLELY on specific, previously obtained information (to the exclusion of other past AND current information). For example, having read in a client's file that he had been diagnosed with Oppositional Defiant Disorder (ODD) and assuming that all the refusal and "shut down" behaviors you're observing in your office are examples of "his ODD."

- **Correspondence bias:** Drawing conclusions about another person's character, traits, and intentions BUT neglecting to take the situation into account when observing them engaging in the behavior. For example, the person cutting you off in traffic is obviously a jerk (a judgment about their character, and that they did this to you on purpose), whereas when YOU cut someone off in traffic, you are more likely to say you did so because of following the flow of other cars, an emergency you were racing toward, or that it was a simple, mindless mistake. Correspondence bias is particularly likely when working with EBD clients because of our vantage point as observers of their "intentional" acting out behaviors.

In the years I've spent working with EBD kids, I've found myself tempted toward certain assumptions. I've caught myself, after watching a particularly dramatic display of child naughtiness during my clinical work—the dropping of "F-bombs" or the erecting of middle fingers in my direction—entertaining words such as "attention-seeking," "manipulative," or "oppositional." I've nodded in agreement with limits that were set that seemed to speak as much to caregiver angst as much as client needs. I've learned to question such responses from the depths of my frustration with a particular kid's behavior. What I realize is that I'm falling prey to universal, yet reversible, limitations of human perception. We are all blocked by our point of view as observers of others' behavior.

Basically, when looking at others, unless there are clear external, environmental causes leaving the person "blameless" (such as the young child with cancer who did nothing to create her situation), we tend to assume (incorrectly) that people's behavior is the inevitable result of their own internal traits. The colleague who walks away from our office in a huff has "an attitude problem." They chose and, therefore, intended this behavior to result. If we're watching someone display "bad" behavior, and there is no clear outside explanation, it is tempting for the bystander to say the person's actions result from some distasteful, personal attributes (for example, laziness). It is easy to see then how our empathy falters. Caring withers when caregivers (often incorrectly) assume people's negative experiences were "deserved." They simply had it coming.

Everyone is prone to such errors in perception. The essence of correspondence bias is the observer's incorrect view of the actor's control over circumstances. In doing so, we ignore the crucial influence of situational or contextual forces on behavior. Think of the last time you were late for work. How would you feel if everyone who noticed your tardiness assumed you were late as a result of some defect in your character? You were not late because of snarled traffic, the burned toast that set off your fire alarm, or your well-groomed, but defenseless, poodle that ran out the door as you opened it. You were late because you're lazy and self-centered. You might feel indignant in response to the rolling eyes and smug looks of your colleagues. You would probably feel misunderstood and want to argue your case to anyone passing judgment. Yes, child clients can act "on purpose" in the moment, but do they really intend the entire pattern—the cycle of anger and anguish that they get locked into time and time again? Perhaps we need to clean the distortive smudges from our perceptual glasses.

Look (To the Fit of Intervention with the Moment)

Even if you merely suspect possible bias (or you're in a situation that has sparked it for you in the past), do the following in order to sidestep tunnel vision and come more fully into awareness of what actually is going on for you, your client and the context of their behavior:

1. Pause and take a slow, deep breath into the belly (sounds simple, but there's no breaking the "bad" of bias without at least one mindful breath!).

2. Ask yourself: What's HERE in my body and mind NOW?

3. Simply NOTICE what answers arrive at your senses and in your thoughts. Don't analyze or ponder them—just observe them.

4. Take another slow, deep belly breath.

5. Perhaps you were about to set a behavioral limit with your client. Perhaps you were going to challenge distortions/irrationality in their thinking and emotions. Instead of launching forward with your interventions, make a practice (after this step of mindful "listening") to LOOK deeply into the moment at hand. Consider inserting at least one (if not more) of the following inquiries into your awareness. These will help open your lens of perception and will safeguard you against the distorting, limiting effect of cognitive bias.

Learn to sidestep clinical tunnel vision by asking the following "W" questions:

- **WHAT** ... matters? ... am I missing? ... is "behind" the behavior? ... would empower growth for this client?

- **WHO** ... will be affected if I merely react? ... needs to know/be looped into this situation so that it's not just me trying to manage it? ... will have their needs met (e.g., the client or ME) if I merely reactively intervene in this moment?

- **WHERE** ... are we now (context)? (The point here is to be aware of your surroundings— perhaps the hallway in front of the client's peers is NOT the best place to unearth the source of her anxiety.)

- **WHY** ... this red-hot moment? ... not let it play out? ... not silence? ... not just *breathe*?

Leap (Into Action)

Now that you've opened up your field of vision a bit, consider how your intervention might shift. Perhaps you'll still do what you were initially intending to do (e.g., set a limit, give advice, redirect, or actively "ignore" the behavior). Perhaps you'll find yourself moving in a different direction altogether. Consider the following "how's" of a more mindful, compassionate leap forward:

■ HOW MIGHT YOU...

> Co-regulate/teach skills to the client instead of merely redirecting, punishing, or waiting out the behavior?

> Compassionately contain their behavior?

> "Eye the prize" as to what might matter at a core, emotional level to this client and let him/her know you're interested in it?

> Model "truth-talking" (e.g., speak from your direct, here and now felt and thought experience)?

Don't *Be* a Tool!
(Be More Than Methods)

Get Oriented

CBT . . . DBT . . . ACT . . . PCIT . . . EMDR . . . PMT . . . ABA . . . The acronyms for the various research-supported and "evidence-based" psychotherapy and behavioral change methods and techniques are numerous (and extremely important!). Learn them, imbed them in your practice arsenal . . . AND be *more* than these tools. In general, and specifically in working with EBD youth, embrace the truth that your work will go from technical to nothing short of transformative when you harness the relationship with your clients and learn to see (and feel) the full field of what's happening in your clinical interactions. Speaking of research: You may have heard that it's not tools and techniques that best predict the outcome of psychotherapy. It's the quality of the therapeutic alliance between therapists and their clients.

You'll leverage that relationship in the service of transformative change for at-risk kids when you learn to see beyond (and behind) their (and your) reactive behavior. When you cultivate mindful, compassionate perspective and communication with EBD clients, you grow the alliance— you produce the conditions for kids to build skills and possibility in their lives.

Listen (To What Actually IS)

The next time your "technical" therapeutic efforts are running aground with an EBD child client, consider the following for rising into a higher, more helpful, alliance-fostering perspective:

- **Anchor yourself in your breathing.** Feel the sensations of the breath in the body as you inhale and exhale.
- **Notice something in your immediate surroundings** or bodily sensations (perhaps the feel of air on your skin, your feet on the floor, or the tick of a clock). Just quickly and silently notice something that is "here and now" *other* than the labels, judgments, and blaming thoughts about the child (e.g., being "a pain," "manipulative," "just looking for attention") that are likely surfacing. Touch base with something there in

the space you're in with your young client OTHER than your intended intervention and the kid's (perhaps less than ideal) reaction.

Look (To the Fit of Intervention with the Moment)

■ **With genuine curiosity, ask yourself: What might they be needing OTHER than this intervention and/or the way I'm delivering it?** What unmet expectation is most important to them? Don't stop with labels of "attention" or "escaping a demand." Although these may have an element of truth, they still blame the kid in a way. Instead ask: And what might be behind *that*? (*Hint:* It will be something along the lines of looking for caring, respect, reassurance, a sense of competence, relief from pain/discomfort, or being connected and belonging to something/someone, and so forth.)

■ **Notice any blankness, push-back, or "but" reactions in your mind and let them pass.** Let go of your agendas and desired outcomes. Hold onto the need behind their behavior as if it's a jewel you've discovered—a hidden treasure others have missed in this kid for a long time. For just a moment, let go of trying to make something happen with your intervention. It's not that your intervention/technique is bad, but perhaps the timing and fit with the needs of the moment in and around the client are less than ideal.

■ **Wonder how this perspective on what's behind things for this child might inform your tool/intervention.** How might you intervene from compassion instead of consternation and an agenda? Perhaps you will lean forward and whisper that you know things are hard and that you want to help them get through this. Or maybe simply loosen and let go of your professional tension and desire for control.

■ **Wonder how this child might benefit from adults informed by compassionate, behind-the-behavior perspective.** If you stay present with them despite their difficulties, what message will that send? If your "tool use" flowed from full consideration of this here-and-now need-based perspective, what might happen to its effectiveness?

Leap (Into Action)

■ **Take in another breath and take a leap in the direction this perspective nudges.** NOW—go ahead and intervene in a non-blaming, non-forcing way. Offer choices or solutions. Give them your sincere caring. Certainly, make it clear that THEY are responsible for their negative behavior and make it clear they are not a bad kid for having used these behaviors to wake people up to the needs behind them. Make it clear that you can't control ANYTHING for this child—they alone choose how they will relate to the moment-to-moment truth of their experience.

The therapeutic relationship flows (and tools click into place) out of open recognition of the inevitable autonomy of every client and the shared responsibility for what happens in the clinical encounter.

Receiving the Message

Get Oriented

This practice is designed to help you "see behind" a child client's behavior, particularly if a particular child client is, has recently, or soon will exhibit challenging behavior with the potential of pressing your emotional buttons.

For the initial run of this practice, sit in a calm, quiet space and sit upright with your eyes gently closed. Call to mind "that" child client. *You know the one*—the kiddo who has really sparked negative reactivity for you (and perhaps others charged with his or her care). See this child's face as vividly as possible and imagine their demeanor, actions, and expressions with as much detail as possible. When you have them firmly in your mind's eye, proceed with the following:

Listen (To What Actually IS)

1. Consider the message of suffering behind every "maladaptive" or "symptomatic" behavior for your child client.

2. Breathe in and allow your client's suffering to come in and down toward the warmth of your own heart.

3. Breathe out and allow that warmth to project out toward your client whether in your presence or not.

4. Continue breathing in this way, noticing what happens to your heart as it regards this young client.

Look (To the Fit of Intervention with the Moment)

- In imagination, visualize a recent exchange with this child, and be curious as to what juncture in the interaction might have provided a subtle (or not so subtle) opportunity for you to hint at your receipt of the true message of his or her behavior.

- Consider a way to let the client know that you have received this message—perhaps a mere acknowledgement that they are struggling/have struggled and have used less than ideal skills for managing it, but nonetheless were trying to do so.

Leap (Into Action)

- Consider an upcoming session or situation in which you will encounter this client. Are you willing to make a commitment NOW to following through on letting the child know that you caught a whiff of what might be driving his or her behavior?

- Don't blame or "tell them," but instead let them know you were thinking about them, and that it makes sense to you that they MAY have been trying to manage some "discomfort"/ "stuck-ness"/"something not fitting right for them" by doing whatever it was they did.

- Let the client see that you don't sweep uncomfortable things under the rug. You circle back and yet do so directly and compassionately.

PRACTICE 1.5

Mutually Exclusive

Get Oriented

Neuroscientific research has demonstrated that brain regions that coordinate the experience and expression of emotion activate *and* inhibit one another.[4] Put another way, the data suggests that when networks responsible for our expression of anger (for example) are tripped and firing, the networks leading to what we collectively call "joy" or even "compassion" are blocked. This may seem intuitive to us as helping professionals, and yet, don't we sometimes intervene (particularly with EBD child clients) in a frustrated/angry state but consider ourselves compassionate and focused on the child's needs? Perhaps it would help for us to experience the disconnect in our brains between these two states of being.

Listen (To What Actually IS)

1. Call to mind a child you are frustrated/angry with in the context of your work.

2. Try to hold onto this negativity AND conjure compassion for the client simultaneously. Really allow yourself to experience the frustration and also imagine the child's silent (or not so silent!) suffering behind their maladaptive behavior.

Look (To the Fit of Intervention with the Moment)

1. Who is experiencing whatever is arising in you at this moment? The "Compassionate Clinician" or the "Reactive Clinician"?

2. Just notice what's showing up in your experience (your bodily senses and your mental thoughts/images).

3. Are you willing and able to regard yourself with compassion for the reactivity/anger, breathe *into* these sensations in your body, and also swing toward a wider perspective that sees the suffering and stuck-ness that led your young client to act in these ways?

4. Notice what happens (and just imagine what's happening in the circuits of your brain) as you allow the shift from reaction to compassion to happen.

Leap (Into Action)

- If you can't be both "clinicians" at the same time, what might the implications be for you in your work with this child?

- What might you do to embody your hard-earned compassion credentials? How might this practice influence your next session or intervention with this client?

Chapter 2

The
Neuroscience
of Connection
and Reactive
Behavior

Brains Are Wired and Conditioned to Connect and React

What (It Is)

n many of the workshops I conduct with parents, educators, and clinicians, I often have them do an activity I first experienced in graduate school. I have pairs of people (often strangers, but it doesn't matter—it works even if they know each other) sit facing one another and do a simple task:

- Hold each other's gaze for just 30 seconds
- And do NOT communicate anything

The activity always unfolds in a similar way, with people chuckling, breaking eye contact and smiling, or looking about awkwardly, as if someone had just spiked the interpersonal punch bowl with something untoward and jarring. Everyone generally agrees they "failed" at the task—that it's basically impossible to *not* communicate when sitting face to face with another human being. And that's sort of the point: Human communication is inevitable. We are always sending messages (verbal and nonverbal) to one another, and we are wired to do so quickly and intensively. Our brains are structured for nuanced and almost instant social messaging.

By the way: People tend to report that this exercise not only feels awkward and unnatural (to hold back from the normal flow of interpersonal exchange), but that it can feel *invasive* to hold another's gaze. From an evolutionary perspective, you can imagine our primal cave-dwelling days and the need to quickly send messages to others in our vicinity to either back up (or get clubbed) or to come hither (and let's share a corner of the cave together). Our brains evolved the wiring to help these messages flow when such an emotional message is intended, which is beneficial to surviving and propagating the biological/genetic aspect of our patterned inheritance.

Deeply understanding this biologically-based connectivity between us helps us build awareness. It helps us cultivate empathy, potentially even for those who provoke us into frustration (child EBD clients). Opening emerges from the deep recognition of our inherent interdependence, our tethering even to those poking reactivity out of us.

Why (It Matters)

So, if we are wired to constantly and unconsciously mirror each other's intentions and emotions, why are we not immediately empathic with everyone (in this case, the kids with EBD we serve)?

One answer is that we are also wired to jump to biased conclusions about the "threat" posed by others' atypical or "negative" behavior (see Pointer 1.2). Another is that our (the child client and YOUR) interactions (as well as between them and their parents/caregivers) are highly conditioned via the principles of operant conditioning (reinforcing and punishing environmental contexts surrounding behavior).

This may seem surprising, but parents and teens also mutually teach each other to escalate things. As with what's happening at a biological level in the brain, this learning—called "operant conditioning"—happens without anyone choosing it. It's largely unintentional and no one's really to blame. That said, you can learn to recognize and interrupt this pattern with the tools presented in this book.

Gerald Patterson and colleagues at the University of Oregon coined the term *parent–child coercive cycle* to describe the pattern in which parent and child mutually influence each other in subtle ways to increase the stuck quality of their interactions and erode communication.[5] Studies ranging over 30 years link these cycles to increased risk of behavioral problems in youth.[6]

In coercive cycles (see the following figures) the caregiver (you/parents) and the child both punish and reinforce each other. And just by way of reminder, "punish" and "reinforce" are used technically to describe how responses to behavior either make that behavior more likely in the future by being rewarding (reinforcement) or less likely by being aversive (punishment).

What's happening here is a process of mutual triggering. The child's anger/reactivity increases, punishing the caregiver. This continues until the caregiver's demand (say, to do a cognitive-behavioral/problem-solving skill-building activity), which is aversive and punishing for the child, is either removed or the caregiver gives the kid what they want (no more "therapy" and a chance to play on the computer). If the caregiver drops the subject, this reinforces and thereby increases the child's angry or acting out behavior. If the clinician or another caregiver gives the child what he or she wants, this reinforces the caregiver's "giving in" behavior, making it more likely in the future.

When or Where (It Applies)

Here's what coercive cycles look like:

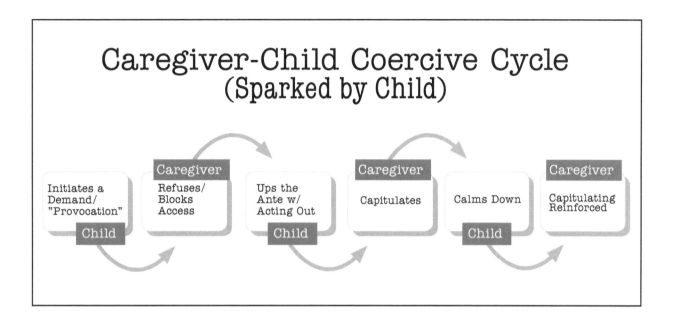

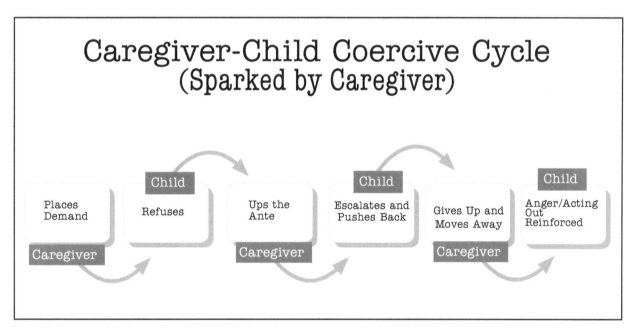

Ask yourself: Do either of these cycles/patterns feel familiar? I'm betting they do—not only for the parents of EBD kids you work with, but in your own interactions with them as well. The key is to learn to look for these patterns proactively and intervene to break them before they solidify (either in your office or in your clients' homes and schools; yes, they happen with teachers and their students, too!). These cycles will emerge when one of you (either the caregiver or the child) introduces a demand that feels unsavory in some respect—a demand on the other's cognition, emotions, or behavior (or all three) that feels less than ideal, if not downright aversive. We talk in other sections of this book how to respond once the cycle has already begun, and limits/redirection of behavior are necessary, but let's focus now on a few tips for preventing (or at least lessening the odds) of these patterns in the first place.

How (To Address It)

It's important to "soften" the presentation of demands on child EBD clients who perhaps have already been conditioned to spark easily into coercive cycling. The key here is to leverage your relationship and the brain-based wiring they were born with to help them hang in as you coach them to more skillfully manage stressful situations in their daily lives.

Try interactive/sharing games/activities at the start or end of sessions. Try not to immediately launch into more taxing/demanding "therapy-like" activities on either end of your session times with kids. Warm them up a bit with a light, fun check-in or ritual of some sort and/or a game, and end the session in a similar fashion. Build the alliance and soften them up for the harder, less preferred work of building coping strategies. If you've sufficiently nudged the relational wiring of kids' brains, they'll hang in a bit more with you when you try to swap out their reactive wiring with more skillful upgrades.

Avoid "chasing the tail" of reactive behavior in kids when you place demands. By this, I mean don't just react to what they say they don't want to do. Instead, introduce something that the two of you can do that (1) validates the at-times un-fun aspect of therapy and (2) restructures the interaction TOWARD something. Don't just distract them with a change in conversation topic; OFFER them an opportunity to do something that both engages/entertains AND teaches them something of value.

Bottom line: Engage and Lead, don't React and Dominate.

Teaching "Hang Time" to Caregivers

Get Oriented

n a famous series of studies,[7] developmental psychologist Ed Tronick asked parents to cease their typical back-and-forth interactions with their infants and abruptly face them instead with blank facial expressions. Through these "still face" experiments, Tronick documented the immense impact—physiological, psychological, and behavioral—of interrupting the normal dance of emotional biologically-necessitated attunement. He and other researchers showed that there are significant negative developmental consequences for kids (and a negative impact for parents) when this attunement is disrupted over time.

You know this already because you feel the impact of the disrupted flow of emotional give-and-take with your clients from time to time. And, of course, if you have kids yourself, you feel the relevance of this all too well. Tronick showed that these interruptions significantly impact the stress levels—and, therefore, the development—of an infant. For the well-being of family members—and for the EBD clients you work with—it's important to shift the emotional balance back toward attunement. Your clients have already likely experienced more attunement disruption than we can imagine. They are very much in need of their caregivers maximizing the quality and quantity of what I like to call "hang time"—attunement-focused interactions that correct and calibrate kids' ability to develop the brain-based attachment capacities they will need throughout their lives for managing distress and forming/maintaining connection with others.

Listen (To What Actually IS)

A key point in coaching your clients' caregivers to practice skills of attunement with their children is to help them become more skillful and intentional observers of behavior. We've all been in public places and enjoyed some degree of "people watching." When you've got parents/caregivers interested and willing to work to build the skills of more effective connection with an EBD child or teen, first ask them (as "homework") to spend time just watching their child's activities. Like a scientist in a laboratory have them spend some of the likely rare moments when they don't have a pressing task at hand just sitting and (without making a show of it and causing paranoia and escalation on the part of the child) observing. I sometimes suggest that caregivers start keeping a journal where they take notes of what is happening around the child (the situation, the context, what others are doing and saying, and what demands are present) with specificity and without judgment or "opinion" labels. Have them apply the same lab-minded objectivity to observing and perhaps writing down specifics of the child's actions in a given situation. Then have them note what happens after these actions (e.g., what do others do/say in response). Behavior analysts would call this collecting data as to the "antecedent conditions" (e.g., context surrounding and predictive of behavior), the behavior itself, and then the "consequences" (the contextual responses following the child's behavior that potentially are either rewarding/reinforcing or punishing/weakening the likelihood that the child will engage in that action again in the future).

Basically, help parents learn to notice the "ABCs" of their child's behavior. They will likely need assistance in collecting this information without the bias/judgment that often comes when you're faced with intense, negative, and frankly upsetting behavior—particularly from your own child. Many parents/caregivers benefit from role-play practice in developing both observational/objectivity skills and the specific skills of "hang time" attunement. Don't allow your own anxiety to lead you down the ineffective path of merely talking about your client's behavior and caregivers' reactions. Have caregivers practice via role play so that you can coach, guide, teach, and support them in the direction of building more skillful attunement–facilitative patterns of behavior.

Obviously, it's ideal to practice these skills *yourself* a number of times (by role-playing and receiving supportive, yet specific feedback from colleagues) prior to attempting to coach caregivers in doing so. With all complex skills you might use either with clients or their caregivers, practice may not ever make for perfection, but it makes for intervention with a much higher probability of being effective.

Look (To the Fit of Intervention with the Moment)

Here are the basics of what caregivers should do during actual planned, scheduled "hang time" sessions with their child. The goal is to build skills of observation and attunement with the emotional needs of the child. Here is a sample of the sorts of instructions and language to use in coaching caregivers in attunement skills during hang time.

1. Carve out at least 10–15 minutes per day to hang out with your child. If possible, establish a regular time for hanging out, a time when you are free from other responsibilities or competing demands.

2. Express interest in joining your child in some sort of leisure activity at home. Don't force the issue. If he or she refuses to allow you to even sit nearby, simply state something like, "Okay, well I'd really like to hang out with you, so I'll look to follow up with you later." And then *definitely* follow up, even if it takes 20 rejections before your child finally says "whatever" and allows you to sit nearby while they play video games. If your child suggests you're just trying to spy or get into their business, then say something like, "Hey, I'm just trying to flip things around between you and me. I'm just looking to show some interest in what matters to you."

3. Ideally, they'll be up for playing a game/puzzle/with a toy that allows for interaction between you. But do not force the issue if they lean toward a more solitary game or activity if that is what their dominant pattern has been, particularly when they are stressed. If not, just sit as your child does whatever it is they like to do.

4. Avoid asking questions, particularly ones that have an emotionally charged, instructive, or "I'm the adult and know more than you" tone. Again, your child assumes you're prying, trying to control things or perhaps judging them in some way. Avoid lecturing or trying to teach. This is *not* a time to instruct your child in any way. Don't try to direct or manage how your child does the activity. Also, don't inquire into sensitive topics during hang-out time. The focus here is not the content of any hot-button issues; it's on the process of your communication with each other.

Leap (Into Action)

1. Practice attunement by:

   › Praising your child's specific actions and positive communication with you. For example, "Nice job clearing that level in the game" or "It's cool how you asked if I wanted to take a crack at this."

   › Summarize anything your child is saying that indicates engagement, even if that's engagement with the activity or topic rather than with you. For example, "So, I'm hearing you say that most people don't have a clue how good you are at this."

   › Describe what your child is doing as if you're a correspondent doing a radio or TV broadcast for a sporting event. For example, "Looks like you're done watching the Kardashians, and now it's time to get down to business with some Xbox® action."

2. Let your child lead the interaction. Practice letting go of trying to control things. Suppress any disdain for your child's preferences or for the irrational, nonsensical passion for a favorite activity. Remember, your child perhaps expects you to show disapproval or sit in judgment. It will send a very powerful message—a message your child will certainly detect—if you refrain from doing so.

3. Whether it's inane gossip shows about overexposed and overpaid celebrities or video games that require more manual dexterity than piloting a fighter jet, it's time you got comfortable hanging out with your child. The point here is to make deposits in your child's emotional bank account that you can draw on later. You want to give small experiences of dedicated attention. Attunement and emotional investment in favorite activities will help your child care more about your relationship going forward. Improvements in the parent–child relationship will increase the prospect for their abilities for learning to get on top of their emotional and behavioral challenges.

Your willingness to hang out with your child with full attention and engagement (and to do so NOT as a reward, but regardless of what their behavior was earlier in the day) will help him or her develop the resilience to hang in there with the difficulties of the change process. This last point is crucial. Hang time is not a reward. It is "non-contingent," offered daily and consistently over time regardless of the behavior earlier in the day or since the last hang-time event. This sends a powerful and corrective message to an EBD child. It basically tells them that "my parent is willing to show up for me even if they are upset about my negative/unskillful behavior from earlier." This message is one of the most important messages of attunement a caregiver can deliver to their child. In and of itself, it is incredibly healing and hope-creating for a child to begin to believe (even though they know their caregiver is upset) that their relationship is worth showing up to consistently.

Cue Kids' Inner Wizard and Teach Them to Sidestep Their Lizard

Get Oriented

As we've discussed, our brains evolved to make us highly responsive (and at times over-reactive) to one another's emotions and behavior. In her "Brainwise" group therapy curriculum for school-age kids, psychologist Dr. Patricia Gorman-Barry provides a great metaphorical tool for helping kids understand and work with the reactivity that's inherent to the brain.[8]

She teaches that all humans have an evolutionarily ancient set of structures (e.g., the amygdala, cingulate cortex) that together are labeled the limbic system. These structures have been present in many animals' brains for many millennia and spark our bodies to react to threat and seek out satisfaction in order to survive. Gorman-Barry refers to this part of the human brain as the LIZARD brain. Even green chameleons I used to find in my bedroom on occasion during my childhood in Daytona Beach, Florida, have rudimentary structures in their brains like these that help them flinch, fight, or flee in response to danger, and "chomp" at something tasty!

What lizards do not have that humans do is a frontal cerebral cortex (sitting squarely behind your forehead). This much more recent evolutionary hardware allows us to channel an inner WIZARD. With these folded nooks and cranial crannies, the human forebrain allows us to problem solve, think, create, imagine, and conjure—perhaps not real magic, but compared to what lizard brains can do, our thinking self does seem rather magical!

Listen (To What Actually IS)

Ask yourself RIGHT NOW:

- Which part of my brain is calling the shots right now—my LIZARD or my WIZARD?

- Notice how readily you know the truth—your brain knows itself!

- Take a slow, full breath into your belly and simply say the label word (either wizard or lizard) to yourself (or out loud).

- Exhale the breath and say which part of your brain is most dominant now (don't worry if the lizard is still clinging to you!).

- Keep breathing in this way, noticing, labeling, and waiting to see what happens. Most people notice that the lizard inevitably (and particularly with the slow, deep breathing) gives way to the wizard. Lizards don't like to hang in with the cooling off effects of belly breathing; they are cold-blooded creatures and need the warmth of rapid breathing and worked-up emotions.

Look (To the Fit of Intervention with the Moment)

In working with your clients, notice a moment of MILD reactivity/frustration during play or another interaction and teach them the previous steps.

It usually works better to have taught clients the metaphors of the brain's wizard and lizard centers in advance. Some kids benefit from actually looking at diagrams of the brain. It can be incredibly normalizing for kids who have often taken a hit to their self-concepts (because of their histories of agitation and acting out) to realize that their brains were wired from the beginning with these structures that spark reactivity—that their parents (and even their therapists) have "lizards," too! If you are working with a child who you believe is suffering underneath the burden of self-blame, this reframing intervention can be helpful and can open them to further coping skills development intervention. Until they believe that others believe their acting out comes from a place of self-protection, their shame will block them from receiving the help they need.

Leap (Into Action)

Model the labeling of the wizard/lizard brain in operation by letting your kids know when your own brain has moved in one or the other direction. Use storytelling to give them examples of how you have struggled with the lizard's reactivity and how you've benefited from the wizard's wise ways. It helps normalize clients' experiences to take the pressure off them and their problem behavior, and gives examples of how you (and others you know and work with) have gone reptilian rigid at times.

Combine the metaphor/labeling with in-session games and coping strategy activities, particularly whenever actual examples of lizard/wizard movements are available. Ask kids to notice which brain center is more effective at managing tough situations. Use role-play practice to help kids experience the benefits of slowing down and letting the wizard wake up and get active. With younger kids, create your own wizard wands and draw pictures or cartoons of lizards getting things stuck. Be kind to animals! Be sure to let kids know that the lizard is not "bad" or "evil." It's part of our brains and is there to help us react to threats and go after stuff we want. But like most lizards, it can't see very far (into the future), and we need the wizard brain to best solve the more complex problems of being a person.

The Self-Regulation Wizard

Mr. Brain Wizard Says . . .

Name It to Tame It

Get Oriented

It was a particularly difficult day. My then 9-month-old daughter had a terrible night and left my wife and me with only a few hours' sleep. Needless to say, we were slow getting up and out the door that morning. Before we left, my wife and I had a "discussion" about who should've gotten up with Celia during the night (we'd been down this road before—these back-and-forths never help solve this issue, and somehow, we yet again veered this way). We barely spoke in the car the rest of the way to work after we dropped our daughter off at daycare.

Then, I was hit by one issue after another once I walked into my office: An upset parent who'd left a voicemail who "urgently" needed to talk to me; a clinician who needed help dealing with a student in crisis; an important meeting I needed to chair that I'd forgotten to put in my calendar. And worst of all, I must have used a ladle to scoop my sugar into my coffee travel mug that morning.

I sat with my face in my hands at my desk for a moment. I was seething with what life had deposited on top of me. My temples were pulsing, and my clock said it was only 9:30. Somehow, I remembered what I'd recommended to clients many times, but usually forgot to do myself. It was a nice therapeutic "nugget" that made sense, but that seemed below me—an experienced therapist. "Name it" (or as I've heard psychiatrist and mindfulness expert Dan Siegel say, "Name it to tame it"). Say to yourself and say out loud what negative emotion you're experiencing, as you're experiencing it, in order to begin getting some distance on it. Somehow, as the clinical wisdom goes, simply labeling a difficult emotional experience allows you to take the reins back, if only briefly.

I'd recommended this emotional labeling to clients for years, but I'm fairly certain I'd never tried it myself. Again, I was a therapist—this simple labeling thing was for my child clients to use. It was "Self-Management 101." I was far beyond such "basic" strategies. I was wrong, because I sat at my desk with distress rippling through me. My mind was electric with ranting, and I was on track for a less than effective, connected, creative day. I needed to return to the basics.

The recommendation comes from a solid foundation. Research has shown that mere verbal labeling of negative emotions can help people recover control.[9] UCLA's Matthew Lieberman, Ph.D., refers to this as "affect labeling," and his fMRI brain scan research shows that this labeling of emotion appears to decrease activity in emotional brain centers such as the amygdala. This dampening of the emotional brain allows its frontal lobe (reasoning and thinking center) to have greater sway over solving the problem du jour.

And this is where mindfulness comes in. Mindfulness gives us that one-second of space as reactive emotions (like anger) are rising up. If we can see the anger, then we don't have to be it—we can mindfully notice the body and mind crackling with reactivity and acknowledge (or "name") our emotions as we're having them. Doing so seems to put them at arm's length. We can see them, and then we can begin to choose. We can choose to act to open ourselves and connect with others, rather than be carried away in a flood of emotional neurochemicals that wash us over the cliff.

Listen (To What Actually IS)

In the coming days, when you find your body and mind hardening with upset (and the more you're aware of exactly how this manifests in you, the better), nudge yourself to attach words to your experience. Often, thinking in terms of the metaphor of your hand in front of your face can be helpful. When you start, you ARE your anger, sadness, fear, whatever. It is your hand over your face. Can't see anything, can you? The emotion is attached to you—it IS you.

As you progressively label your emotion, creating more and more "distance" between the raw emotion and "you," the observer (sparking awake in your frontal lobe) begins to see things more clearly. The emotional "hand" moves farther away from your thinking and reasoning mind's eye.

Here's a possible domino effect of reactive thoughts that might show up for you:

- Event occurs...
  - Body stiffens, clenches...
    - "I can't believe this!"/"They are so wrong!"/"This shouldn't be!"
      - "I am angry/sad/frustrated/humiliated."
        - Body stiffens, clenches more
          - "I'm going to let them have it!"

And now, insert the following instead, just AFTER the body first stiffens, surges, or in some way alerts you that upset is here:

- "My body is telling me I'm angry or sad." (deep, slow breath in)
  - "I'm having thoughts that this is upsetting." (slow exhale out)
    - "Anger...anger...anger..." (deep, slow breath in)
      - Body slows down (slow exhale out)
        - "Sad...sad...sad..." (deep, slow breath in)

Look (To the Fit of Intervention with the Moment)

Notice the "distance" that develops as you label your way away from the event and step away from the raw emotion itself. Instead of reacting and either lashing out or shutting down, you (in a matter of seconds) can ignite your frontal lobe, slow your body and mind, and choose your response. You can connect with your experience, as well as the possibilities around you. Instead of digging a deeper hole, you can climb out of the episode.

Leap (Into Action)

Practice this labeling whenever you can. Don't be discouraged when you find yourself swept away in the emotional currents. Our emotional reflexes run deep (inside the brain), and change comes only with significant practice and patience. Your amygdala will continue to flare at times. You can, however, get better at catching yourself. Labeling emotion helps you create the distance for choice to emerge.

I still argue with my wife about who should go pick up my crying kids. I catch my rigid, "she's so out of line" thinking more than before, and I put it out at arm's length. More than ever before, I can choose to do something that binds us together instead of blasting us apart.

And if all that mindful labeling doesn't work, as a husband, I've learned to simply stop talking and go clean something ...

Open-Handing Your Stress

Get Oriented

We all grip our thoughts and emotions too tightly from time to time, particularly in stressful situations. Work with EBD child clients can be especially hard. Their in-session behavior is at times tough to manage; they trash your office, and it can feel as though things are not going anywhere positive. Whatever it is, all of us get stressed and grip ourselves so tightly that things shut down and close up. This activity is a way to practice taking tension, watching it, and slowly opening to our experience until things change on their own.

Listen (To What Actually IS)

1. Lay your hands gently on your thighs (palms up).

2. Take a deep breath. Feel your body in the place you're sitting.

3. When you're ready, close your eyes and focus your attention on the sensations of either your left or your right hand.

4. Ball your hand into a fist and hold it as tight as you can for several seconds. Release your hand. Repeat this process a few times.

5. Notice the difference between the tension and the feeling of release.

6. Now, allow your hand to lay open on your lap. Notice the sensations showing up there.

7. Try not to simply "think about" your hand, but instead, sense the pulsing, the tingling, itching, whatever might be present in the moment. Continue noticing your mind on what your open hand senses, whether it's a sensation in the hand, another part of your body, or even a passing thought.

8. Notice how all these experiences come, go, and change on their own.

9. Your hand is open and can hold whatever shows up—so can YOU. The stress of the moment shows up and, with presence, you can hold it gently, and it will come and go on its own.

Look (To the Fit of Intervention with the Moment)

Try remembering this activity during challenging interactions. No one needs to know, but you can silently tense and release your fist and let the taut aspect go just like the tightness in your hand will as you silently watch, breathe, and do the best you can in that situation.

Leap (Into Action)

Try repeating phrases to yourself as you move forward with your day, such as:

- ■ "Tension will show up as I deal with this . . . I can choose to let it go."

You might also utilize this practice enough that you can develop the habit of silently curling your fingers on one hand into a subtle fist while it lies on your lap. You can intentionally draw all your body and mind's stress into that hand on a slow, deep inhale, and then open your hand with an exhale. Look at your client (or the situation at hand) as you do, and choose to "let go" of the tension and reactivity. Ask the following of yourself:

- ■ "How might I compassionately and directly lean into this moment and lead things?"

Chapter 3
Emphasizing the Validity of Children's Inner Experience

Equivalence of Experience

What (It Is)

Decades ago, psychologist Martin Seligman documented the phenomenon of *learned helplessness*.[10] Learned helplessness is a feeling of complete and absolute resignation in the face of negative inputs that do not seem to stop no matter what you do. Does this sound familiar? It has for many of the EBD clients (and their families) I've worked with. When faced with an onslaught of anger, anxiety, and acting out (or in) for weeks, months, or even years, it is completely understandable to sink into a feeling of hopelessness or defeat.

When pain is here and now, it's important to rest *into it* rather than trying to fight it off. Do what you can to address and change a tough situation. Beyond that, acceptance—not resignation—can help you ride out the pain.

Here's the thing: It's not just our EBD clients and their families who need to learn about mindful acceptance of the "truth" of their painful experience. We need to learn to acknowledge ours as well and (very importantly) recognize that our truth is equivalent to that of any client.

What I mean by this is that in a given situation and interaction between two or more people, each person is entitled to their own capital "T" truth—the bodily sensations, emotions, thoughts, and mental images that are happening. When we're with one another, there are multiple "big T's" in the room, and things are going to go much, much better in the communication between folks if this obvious and indisputable fact is acknowledged by all parties.

When you're thinking or feeling something, you're thinking and feeling something . . . and so am I . . . and so is anyone else in that situation (and around the world at that moment!). Telling someone that they are NOT thinking and feeling whatever they are while they are doing so is the most incredible form of delusion and attempted existential burglary I can imagine. It's the ultimate "alternative fact" to deny someone the experienced validity of their truth.

Why (It Matters)

Particularly when we're living or working with someone (*hint, hint*: children and teens with emotional and behavioral disorders) who can exhibit varying degrees of noxious, perplexing, off-putting, and intensely draining behaviors, it's tempting to veer toward a bit of nay-saying as to the validity of their thoughts, sensations, and emotions. As tempting as this may be, to go down that rabbit hole in pursuit of "small t" truth (e.g., a "fact" that multiple people might agree upon regardless of the big T experience of the person involved) is to spark the beginning of the end of an effective communication or intervention sequence with that child. Would you prefer to be right or would you rather be effective?

Acceptance and recognition of the inescapable validity of personal, big T truth is basically another way to look at mindful communication. Acceptance is the full, nonjudgmental choice to rest in your moment-to-moment sense experience. The classic metaphor for understanding acceptance is that of quicksand. If you fall into a pit of quicksand, you have to consciously not do what your body and mind reflexively want to do—that is, flail about in panic. Instead, you have to lie back and rest into the quicksand, maximizing your surface area and floating. Doing so opens possible solutions for actually getting out of the trap you're in. If you're flailing about, you're much more likely to miss that stranger in the distance who could come over and yank you out. That's acceptance. And that's what's missing if we're working and acting from a foundation of our perspective being more accurate or valid than the client's. They can feel this hierarchy, this I'm "more right than you," and it will block their willingness to work with you.

When or Where (It Applies)

This principle is most important for you to remember in the moments when you are *convinced* that the client is doing or saying something completely maladaptive and irrational. Honoring the client's truth does *not* mean you agree with their logic, their behaviors, or their decisions. You may disagree with the conclusions and implications their thinking and feeling have on their behavior, and you may very much take issue with the negative effects these behaviors are having on others (and themselves), but you are only going to be effective to the degree that an EBD child or teen client can surmise that you buy into the fact that he or she is thinking or feeling whatever they happen to have been experiencing. You must start at the "A" point of the client's experience before helping them move toward the "B" point of changing their behavior. I wish it were possible to wave a therapeutic wand and make their big and little "T's" match up and meet some ideal universal standard, but it's not. In fact, I don't wish that because such a world would make us all the same, would be extremely dull, and last (and very importantly) we'd all be out of our jobs!

So be on the alert in your every work interaction for your temptation to call "fake news" on a client's truth of experience. Yes, help them develop more skillful behaviors, but first, let them feel felt: Make sure they can feel that you truly honor their thoughts and feelings as *having happened*. The greatest injustice any of us can experience is the absolute denial of our actual experience. Allow for their experience to co-exist with yours, and you're on your way to significant potential for positive change

How (To Cultivate It)

In order to build your ability to overtly honor the truth of EBD clients' experience, consider the following contemplations. Write your favorites on index cards and tack them up in your work space where you'll see them often—particularly during clinical interactions with kids. Let them prompt you out of reactive "expertise," or high and mighty "rightness," and let them prompt you to come back down to the unarguable truth of the equivalence of your experience with theirs.

- Being right or being with?

- Feeling felt or feeling dealt (with)?

- What am I missing in this situation?

- What am I assuming?

- Drill down to their truth or climb up on my pedestal?

- Eye to eye or eye for an eye?

- Win/lose, win/win or NO CONTEST?

- What's here now that is unarguable?

- Big T progress or little t stuck-ness?

- Let your Big T show ... (I'm looking into having T-shirts made with this one!)

Thinking Space

Get Oriented

Cognitive psychotherapists call for clinicians to challenge the rational validity of extreme or "distorted" thinking. Although there is a great deal of research data to support the general effectiveness of cognitive-behavioral therapies for children, when we're talking about work with kids with significant EBDs, it is often helpful to have additional (or alternative) tools in the box for helping kids manage their sharper-edged, most maladaptive thinking. Mindfulness skills are helpful in this regard.

As opposed to nudging kids to refute their own thoughts of "My teacher sucks and has it out for me" or "My parents never give me what I want," you instead help kids use their own moment-to-moment experience to see that these actually are . . . just thoughts (words and images/mental pictures) passing through the mind's eye. Kids with EBDs will sometimes bristle with reactivity when they sense therapists challenging the validity of their thinking. We can sidestep this issue by teaching them to NOTICE without BECOMING their thoughts. *They* get to decide where to place their attention.

Listen (To What Actually IS)

Here are the basic steps for practicing mindfulness of thinking. Practice it yourself and then (and only then—and only after you've practiced a LOT on yourself), try teaching it to the child clients you work with.

1. Take a stuck, upsetting, and/or extreme thought (about yourself, others, or situations) and notice it as a complete thought. Perhaps write it out and/or draw a picture of it just as it sounds as you're thinking it. In particular, aim for the thoughts that are "sticky"— the always/never/should/must/need to/finger-pointing/forceful/black-white/extreme in some way thoughts.
2. Now add the following to the beginning of the thought: "Right now, I notice myself *having* the thought that . . ."

3. Write the thought out on an index card or sticky note (the latter are great because of their "stickiness") and write/draw the thought. Place it as close to or as far from your face as it "feels" when you're actually thinking it (*hint:* Extreme/upsetting thoughts are often right up on top of your face, as if they ARE you).

4. Keep adding the phrase, "Right now I'm having the thought that..." to the beginning of the thought (and say it out loud, over and over) and move the card/sticky note in closer or out away from your face as the FEELING of the thought (its sting and stickiness) changes (if it does). What happens to the feel of the thought as you "play" with it like this?

5. Do things get more stuck, extreme, rigid, or in some way negative, or do things open up, loosen up, get clearer? Is there more or less room to make choices and see different ways to view the situation?

The goal here is to practice any or all of these techniques for shifting from a rigid, absolute frame for the thought and fostering a new, more flexible relationship with one's mental experience. This requires a lot of practice and must become a habit to be of real benefit. Such a habit will do much to give a measure of psychological freedom amid the most challenging provocations and actions.

Look (To the Fit of Intervention with the Moment)

Some important pointers for teaching EBD child clients about mindfulness of their thoughts follow:

- Don't debate with the child about their thoughts. Let go of the "convincing" or "being right" agenda. How often do these EBD child clients pause after we try to convince them to think differently and say, "Hey! You're right! Thanks so much for pointing out how I should look at things!"?

- PLAY with mindful thinking using props and experiential activities that will engage and sustain the attention of kids.

- Make sure you're willing and able to model mindfulness of your own thinking on a regular basis. Say out loud, "I'm over here noticing my own mind saying X" and perhaps toss in how you are just now noticing how stuck and tight that feels when you think that thought or something in that direction. Modeling this flexible deftness of your own inner witness helps normalize kids' experience and also fosters a stronger therapeutic relationship (always a good thing!).

Here are additional ways to mindfully "play" with extreme thinking. And be careful here—by playing with kids' thinking, you are not making light of their upset or pain or disagreeing with the content of their thoughts. You're not mocking them. You're merely suggesting that they take the reins of their attention and SEE/LISTEN TO thoughts more flexibly and with increasing awareness in order to put them more in control.

- Think: "Thanks, Mind, for coming up with...(insert the thought here)."
- Take a breath and mentally "place" the thought over in the corner of the room. Visualize what shape, color, size, movement, and sounds would describe it. Just watch it there in the corner for a few breaths.

- Think the thought *very* slowly, as if the recording is messed up and playing back in slow motion.
- Regard the thought as if it's a car passing you . . . as YOU, a bystander, are merely watching from the safe distance of the sidewalk.

Leap (Into Action)

In my own work with EBD child clients, I've noticed that things go much better, kids (and I, as well!) feel better, and I'm much more effective when we SEE thoughts without BEING them. Teach your clients to see their thinking as a tool in and of itself. Thoughts (even the really stuck/sticky ones aren't inherently bad; they are a means of trying to make sense of things, to keep a threatened and distressed thinker from perhaps feeling more pain. The problem is that these thoughts harden, stick around, and block clear, longer term, and often more effective problem solving and self-management.

Teach kids to test it out for themselves by doing "thought experiments"—not the standard kind, but actual experiments where they notice the feel, shape, sound, and workability of thoughts in their own experience by listening to and watching them closely moment to moment. Teach them to do so, and they will see that thoughts are not, by themselves, who they ARE—not solid things that can weigh them down and suck them in. Teach them to relate to the thought so that it doesn't bind them up.

Seeing Your Sgt. Mind

If you were to describe what your own internal "Sgt. Mind" looks and sounds like, how would you do so? Although it might seem a little silly, it can be very helpful to start practicing the skill of separating upset/agitated thoughts, emotions, and actions from who you are at the core—the "you" who wants a life that feels good and is going somewhere important.

Who is Sgt. Mind for you?

- What does your Sgt. look like physically?

_____

- What sort of "tone" does Sgt. Mind use with you?

_____

- Does his voice ever sound like any other voices you hear?

_____

- What sorts of things does he say about:

  › You?

  _____

  › Others?

  _____

  › The world?

  _____

  › Your future?

  _____

Befriending the Good, the Bad, and the Not So Pretty

Get Oriented

How many times have you heard a child or teen client put themselves down or compare themselves to peers and assume they're coming up short? Clients struggling to manage their behavior are especially likely to have histories significant for very low self-esteem and self-talk that swims in negativity and assumptions of "less than" status. Helping EBD child/teen clients make progress often requires that you help them learn to hang out with all aspects of themselves—to more accurately acknowledge their challenges and learn to find evidence of strengths and possibilities as well.

Try the following activity with *yourself* first and then consider using it as a way to help your clients learn to simultaneously touch (and befriend) all parts of themselves, even if some of them could stand some upgrading! We all can benefit from greater self-acceptance, and in working with EBD youth, we *perhaps* (and only very occasionally) assess ourselves as lacking. Your best work lies on the other side of a heaping dose of self-compassion!

Listen (To What Actually IS)

Take a stopwatch and sit in a place where you won't be distracted. Have kids think of all domains of their lives—school/academic, peers, family, sports, and so forth. Suggest that they focus on skills or behaviors that can be seen versus traits or qualities that we tend to lump together for ourselves or others. If you're doing the activity yourself, think of your role, professional activities, and intervention efforts as a clinician.

Time yourself, and for a full two minutes, write every *positive* attribute, skill, or achievement that you can think of about yourself. Write as quickly as you can without stopping to think about the accuracy of anything that comes to mind.

_____

_____

_____

_____

You probably guessed the next step. Time yourself again (two minutes), this time writing every _negative_ habit, action, or pattern you can think of about yourself. Ready, set, go!

_____

_____

_____

_____

Look (To the Fit of Intervention with the Moment)

Look over your lists, count the number of things you listed for both positive and negative attributes, and list them here:

Positive: _____   Negative: _____

Spend time with kids (or colleagues as a group or in contemplation with yourself) and consider each of the following questions:

- What do you notice in comparing your positives and negatives? Is one list longer than the other, and what does this suggest as to your degree of compassion for yourself in your daily life?
- How does it _feel_ to look over both lists? Do you find yourself getting distracted or wanting to push this activity away?
- Are you willing to take a deep breath and hang out with both of them just as they are?
- Might the length and nature of your lists change based on whether you've just gotten in trouble or had a tough episode?
- Is it possible to hold all of these items _right now_ as merely experiences, thoughts, emotions, and memories of past situations that you might learn and grow from?
- Is there any possible advantage or positive thing that developed over time from any of your negatives? A relationship that came about, an opportunity that showed up, or some way in which you grew/got more skillful as a result?

Leap (Into Action)

Take this exercise a step further. Read your lists out loud (to yourself or even to a group). Don't read the items as you've listed them. Instead, read them by alternating the positives with the negatives. Read back and forth between the lists, joining each item with the word *and*. (For example: "Really studying hard for my last math test" *and* "Blaming others for things I actually did.")

Keep breathing slowly and also slowly read over each item from both lists—again, linking the positives and negatives with the word "and."

What happens *right now* to your feelings and willingness to hang in with hard things when you can hang out with memories of skillful and unskillful actions and choices you've made? Going forward, try talking to (and about) yourself in this balanced way—focus on behaviors (not judgmental labels) and be able to notice both the good, the bad, and the not-so-skillful—even in the same breath!

PRACTICE 3.4

Do a Wants and Needs Assessment

Get Oriented

Clinicians are quite used to assessing what their clients need. It's what we do when we render diagnoses and put together treatment plans. This is a necessary and valuable process, without which our interventions would be little more than poorly-timed advice-giving and warm, therapeutic comfort food without much effective, nourishing value. It is a mistake, however, to hammer away at what clients "need" without simultaneously attending to what they want. What would you rather—be absolutely accurate in preaching what the client needs or actually have a client who *returns* to engage the work? There's no helping without someone available to be helped.

Ideally, interventions hit the sweet spot of considering both the needs and wants of clients. Look for the overlap and hammer away at addressing these junctures, and you'll likely see not only some degree of client engagement, but effectiveness and progress as well.

Oh, and by the way: Doing wants and needs assessments are not only crucial for you to do with your clients. You need to do it for yourself as well (whether you want to or not!). Clinicians who assess and intervene at the sweet spot of needs/wants for both themselves and their clients are doing the balancing act required for moving forward in this high-wire act called clinical work with EBD children.

Listen (To What Actually IS)

To begin your own wants and needs assessment, it can help to take stock of what you're doing (and not doing) to keep yourself resilient and vibrant as a professional. In his 2008 book *The Resilient Clinician*, Robert Wicks presented an interesting list of causes of burnout.[11] Though these obviously require more of an empirical stamp of approval before we can view them as definitive, these factors (listed in part here) make sense and put a frame on the need for the skills we'll be building together. As you scan the list, look for glimmers of yourself. Place a check mark by any you recognize.

_____ Inadequate quiet/down time
_____ Vague criteria for success

_____ Guilt over failures and for taking time to nurture one's needs

_____ Unrealistic ideals

_____ Inability to deal with anger or other interpersonal tensions

_____ Extreme need to be liked by others

_____ Neglect of emotional, physical, and spiritual needs

_____ Poor community life and/or unrealistic expectations regarding support from others

_____ Working with others who are burned out

_____ Extreme powerlessness to effect change

_____ Being overburdened with administrative work

_____ Lack of appreciation by colleagues and superiors

_____ Prejudice or discrimination

_____ High conflict in one's personal life

_____ "Savior complex" regarding helping others

_____ Seeing waste in projects that seem to have no relation to helping clients

_____ Not having the freedom or ability to remove oneself from frequent stressful events

_____ Overstimulation, isolation, or alienation

Take out a journal and list the items you've placed a check mark next to. Without judgment, labels, or negativism, describe the actions you take (or don't take) that contribute to these issues. Describe the actions of others with whom you interact.

Now that you've done this, we're going to pause in this assessment practice activity to go back to considering the wants and needs of a specific EBD client in your caseload. Conjure a specific client and call them vividly to mind. Review recent notes if it will help you get the details of their behavior, life and treatment history, and response to intervention firmly in mind.

To help you bring the client vividly into your mind's eye, take a few moments and do the following visualization exercise.

Look (To the Fit of Intervention with the Moment)
Clinician as Client

- Please close your eyes . . . draw in a deep, slow breath. Slowly release it. Another deep, slow breath. Release it, and as you do, recognize that for the next few moments _You are no longer you_. You did not graduate with an advanced degree in mental health. You have not been a professional helper. You do not claim specialized knowledge of how people come to be stuck in their lives and how people can go about getting unstuck. You are not sitting in the chair in your office you are more than used to—the perch that is your vantage point on the lives of those you are trying to help. That chair is empty.

- Deep, slow breath. Eyes closed. You're watching that empty chair. You're sitting across from it. You are _that_ child client (or their parent) . . . the one who hits the buttons of the therapist who sits in that empty chair. Think of him or her. You are sitting in _their_ chair.

- What are you wearing? How are you sitting? What are the habits of movement? What are the words that tend to accompany the breaking away of eye contact? Of glances to the floor or ceiling? What are the idiosyncrasies? For now, they are yours.

- Deep, slow breath. Eyes are still closed. The chair across from you is still empty. You're still in the other one. The one visited by so many people—most of whom you look forward to helping. But again, you are *that* child client (or parent). The one who hits buttons.

- From this chair, what is it you most want? What matters? What do you hope for out of the next 50 minutes? Let yourself wonder. Really get curious about what you want in your life—what changes feel crucial to you.

- Do you feel that the person who sits in that empty chair *fully* gets you? Understands what your experience of life is like?

- How does it feel to come in each week to talk to the person who sits in that chair about what is not working in your life? What are the blackest thoughts and feelings? The thoughts and feelings you actively shove away when you sit with this therapist?

- Did you plan to come here each time to hit their buttons? To struggle against them? To make them feel incompetent and ineffective? To make them withdraw? To spark the same feelings in them you cannot have for yourself? Did you intend any of this?

- Do you want to be happy? Do you want to be free of pain and suffering? What are you hoping to get from this person sitting across from you?

- Deep, slow breath. You are *you* again. The helper back in the usual chair. You have your diplomas. Your specialized knowledge. Your years of clinical experience. You see *that* child client (or their parent) coming into your office, sitting down across from you. Open your eyes . . .

Now, proceed with the following questions, again using your journal if you need more space to write out your reflections.

■ Client NEEDS I think should be addressed in treatment:

_____

_____

_____

■ What do I think the client WANTS to address by coming to treatment?

_____

_____

_____

■ Where is the overlap between wants and needs (the "sweet spot")?

_____

_____

_____

■ Are there any NEEDS that are more my own than the client's?

_____

_____

_____

Now, pause and switch gears again. Go back to your own wants and needs—about both your professional and personal life.

Leap (Into Action)

Look at the Venn diagram on page 65, and insert "Clinician" where it says "Client." What are your needs (personal and professional)? What do you want from your work life? What might be the overlap/sweet spot that addresses both the wants and needs? Are any of your listed needs less your own and more those of others that you've assumed in some way?

The series of inquiries in this practice is easy to rush through or slough off altogether. Do so at your professional peril! This is actually one of the more important practices in this book. The perspective and compassionate accuracy it provides will be well worth the small investment in time and effort. Again, the key question is ... *Are you willing*?

Patience as Self - (and Other) Care

Get Oriented

We've all had it drilled into us since childhood that "patience is a virtue." It's as though we, especially in modern, Western society, need to be convinced—we need proof that patience figures large in our lives. Patience somehow has accrued a reputation of a "nicety" among positive attributes—a sense of its being desirable but not crucial to "success" in our Western Times-Square-meets-Wall-Street world. Patience is great, but other qualities that drive it home, seal the deal, and score points are preferred.

Merriam-Webster defines *patient* as "able to remain calm and not become annoyed when waiting for a long time or when dealing with problems or difficult people." There isn't much nuance to this definition.

Though it sounds great to "remain calm" (I'm thinking of someone yelling this at people during a stampede into an Apple® store for the newest i-ware) and to "not become annoyed" in the face of "problems" or "difficult kids," there's not much of a sense of what this is internally, let alone how it's done.

Developing one's skills for mindfulness is how you build patience, and it's very important for self-care. For those in a helper role with EBD child clients, practicing and building patience is also good for building your ability to be truly helpful to clients.

Listen (To What Actually IS)

Here are some suggestions for going beyond a passive view of patience to making it the crucial skill it is—one that you actively build into your daily life.

Do the following to work on building your patience "muscle":

1. **Ask yourself: Does your indignation toward another person feel good?**

   Does it make things more do-able and manageable? Does it boost or block the mind? How might letting it fester and fly out negatively impact us and others? Basically, what are the costs of feeding your angry impatience?

2. **Ask yourself: How might you learn something from this "transgressor"?**

Without intending to, how might they be teaching you about the edges, the boundaries of your capacity for patience? You don't have to like the pain they've set in motion for you, but are you willing to be at all *grateful* for this opportunity to expand your patience and capacity for well-being?

3. **Make your goal to ride out reactive urges or impulses public to others.**

Make yourself accountable for practicing patience. Here's where I'd recommend modeling this by talking to your clients (with good judgment as to what you're disclosing and the possible ramifications for the client). Give them examples of how you (in the past or even currently) are working to build patience with others.

4. **Stack the deck.**

Try not to put yourself in situations where you'll need to resist urges or fight impulses when you're fatigued and depleted. Rely on rituals and routines for times when you're likely to be fried and impatient (e.g., toward the end of your workday or in mornings before you've had your first caffeinated infusion!).

Look (To the Fit of Intervention with the Moment)

Impatience pulls the rug out from under our best and most well-intentioned interventions as professionals. It seems to especially do so with those who matter to us most and/or in situations in our work (such as with EBD youth) when our emotional buttons are being hit (e.g., we're feeling stuck and ineffective, thrown/confused as to what to do, flooded with anxiety or anger).

When we flare with frustration, or when we shut down and check out with others, it's because we're losing touch with what mindfulness practices teach. Look for moments to practice patience, and coach your clients to look for these moments as well. By anticipating these triggering situations, and having mindfulness tools at the ready, you (and your young clients) will have a much better chance of sidestepping overreactions that have negative consequences and foster downturns in self-regard and relationships. Look for situations in which the following emotional hurdles are emerging in the road of daily life:

1. Desire/Wanting immediate (or rapid) satisfaction
2. Hostility/Wrestling against others' behavior
3. Fatigue/Wilting of the mind and body
4. Restlessness/Worrying about what might happen next
5. Doubting yourself and others' support of you

Impatience pulls the rug out from under our best and loving intentions and is most likely to start yanking when these inner patterns get sparked inside us (and the clients we work with). We basically get impatient when we get stuck internally on a false sense that things should be (and feel) other than they actually do in a given moment. Patience is saying "this too shall pass" to yourself and the world. Pain and discomfort will move through and away from us if we get aware, watchful, and ... patient.

Leap (Into Action)

In my own practice, and for those I work with as a clinician, there are three mindful components to building patience:

1. Cultivating acceptance of what is actually here in the present moment

2. Getting clear around the very real fact that everything changes

3. Not getting stuck on believing that you are separate, an "island unto yourself"

Patience may not be flashy, but it *is* crucial to well-being and effectiveness. And it's not something only the Dalai Lama, Gandhi, or Mother Teresa can do (e.g., notions of certain people having the "patience of a saint"). Patience is what modern psychological and brain science would support, and it's what you can do while you're waiting for the next thing—the end of the meeting, your driveway at the conclusion of a long commute home from work, the salivation and smell of dinner served, the anticipation of a lofty goal's attainment or, dare I say, a "challenging" child client's departure from one's office.

Chapter 4
Foundational Skills
of Clinical
Presence

Your Mindful Presence Is the Greatest Gift

What (It Is)

Much has been written in recent years about the benefits and efficacy of mindfulness practices. Numerous studies (well over a thousand) document that developing the skills for centering one's mind on the present moment can change physical structures in the brain involved in attention, monitoring action, and regulating emotion[12] and can lead to benefits such as increased tolerance of stress and physical illness, as well as reductions in conditions such as anxiety, pain, and depression.[13] It has also been linked to decreased health care costs.[14] Mindfulness is no mere fad or neat psychological parlor trick.

What exactly is mindfulness? It is not something requiring religious beliefs or mystical rituals. It is not a "weak" or passive response to the difficult aspects of your work. Very importantly, mindfulness is not something you do in order to achieve deep relaxation, especially in the midst of classroom chaos or intensity with a difficult client. Although mindfulness practice, done consistently, may help generate feelings of relaxation more consistently, it's not realistic to aim for flower-filled meadows of bliss.

Mindfulness, in the context of clinical work with EBD children and youth, is your skillful management of "presence"— allowing yourself to fully contact the understandable and inevitable thoughts, sensations, and emotions in yourself that arise in the moment during your clinical work. Actors are known for their "stage presence"—their capacity for resonating deeply with their character's role, as well as their fellow actors and the audience. Presence is crucial to clinicians as well. When we resonate deeply to ourselves, the situation at hand, and our clients, we are fully present— we are leveraging awareness of thought, feeling, and behavior in a way that is felt as a meaningful presence for clients.

Why (It Matters)

It goes without saying that clinical work is a challenging, at times overwhelmingly, difficult profession. Whether it's an anxious or acting-out child client or just a day where the demands of treatment planning, collateral calls, and administrative meetings seem endless, the job requires more than its share of the clinician's emotional and mental faculties. Intervening effectively and with transformative impact requires full engagement from you. Training and experience are crucial, but it all falls short without mindfulness of what the moment brings to bear in your office. It is important that you cultivate the foundation of awareness to hold whatever arises and lean in toward it in order to make true progress for these clients happen.

Mindfulness is the filter through which all your interactions and intervention efforts pass. What comes out in your in clinical work is either purified or tainted by the clarity of your awareness in every moment. Where is your mind *now*?

When or Where (It Applies)

What we're talking about with mindful presence with EBD clients is not a "sometime" skill—something you pull out like a calculator or, these days in particular, an iPad®. Mindfulness is not a "strategy," and it's about as "sometime" as gravity. Check in with your experience—how much of the time does gravity not apply to your daily activities? Mindfulness is similarly universal. It is there to be used; if not, you miss opportunities to take in what's there in yourself, your office, and your clients and respond in the present moment with teaching that not only informs but also transforms.

Here we're addressing a need: how clinicians can go about developing their own daily mindfulness practice in order to "be like gravity" with their EBD clients in each and every session—to be fully present, engaged, and attuned to these, at times, tough-to-attune-to kids and the sequelae they bring. Mindfulness practices are not about helping you merely "pay attention" more but are meant to become part of who you are as a person and professional.

Ask yourself: Am I really a "clinician" apart and distinct from my clients? Clinician requires that you are fully there with your clients, in every moment looking to create the "clinician" in them. There's no separation. Like it or not, you and your clients need each other.

Clients will occasionally point out the inaccuracies, the flaws in your interventions and approach to your work. What will you do in those moments of embarrassment and uncertainty?

Colleagues will upstage you in their efforts to gain the favor of others and accolades. How will you handle the resentment and frustration?

Some clients and some sessions will bore you to tears. What will you do with the press of your aching, yawning thoughts?

Young minds will sit in front of you day after day, eager to be doing many things, most things, more than what you're asking of them to do in the course of therapy. Where will your own mind go, and what will you make of the uphill feel, the endlessly steep angle of your work as a clinician?

How (To Cultivate It)

There are endless books, CDs, classes, and retreats where you can take a deep dive into learning to meditate. Instead of listing them here, consult the Appendix at the back of this book for various options. If you're looking for a few simple pointers for beginning to cultivate a mindfulness practice at this very moment, then by all means do the following:

- Sit comfortably.

- Bring your attention to the feelings/sensations of your breathing.

- When your mind drifts away (and it will many times), simply and gently bring your focus back to the feel of your breath.

- Repeat.

My friend, colleague, and fellow mindfulness trainer, Tara Healey of Harvard Pilgrim Healthcare, likes to elicit a commitment from mindfulness practice newbies—sometimes simple and manageable in order to help people get a valid feel for what meditation is all about.

It's a simple formula ... **3 x 3 x 3**

- 3 minutes of practice a day

- 3 days a week

- 3 weeks total

That's an "ask" that most of us can commit to and follow through on. Again, consider the crucial question in this book ... *Are you willing?*

Eyeing the Prize in Kids

Get Oriented

This skill is perhaps the most obvious and the easiest to assume that you already possess the necessary skills. Most clinicians already believe (rightly so) that they connect emotionally with their child clients. Most already know to "catch 'em being good," praise positive behavior, and build relationships with children whenever possible.

Think of times when people have praised you—sometimes you liked it, and sometimes it may have left you feeling patronized. There's a level of skill in connecting with kids that goes beyond praise. A former supervisor of mine called it "prizing." Prizing goes beyond any sense of hierarchy or being the well-adjusted professional and is more about the authentic relating of one person to another. It's a reminder to us as professionals to let child clients occasionally see that we, as people, really value what we see them doing—as if their efforts to change are a gift we've happened upon.

Prizing goes beyond praise. It lets kids know not only that you see something good they are doing, but it also adds the sentiment that their actions matter to you. It's looking at the child and saying, "Hey, I noticed your effort back there, and that was really cool, and very impressive to me/really made me feel good/helped me to see things differently."

Children can certainly respond well to being praised by adults. They can also react negatively when they feel they are being "manipulated" with praise to do things the adult wants and/or when they perceive the praise as being forced or inauthentic. Opposed to praise is the concept of "prizing" client behavior. This is a relationship-building skill that can do much to let clients know that their efforts are noticed. It also models authenticity and goes a long way toward helping clients build courage for connecting with their resilience and capacity to hang in with challenges.

Here are a couple of other advantages of prizing: It makes you matter more to the child and, thus, they will be more likely to take input and direction from you. It's also "contagious." It builds a culture of connection for others.

Listen (To What Actually IS)

Anticipate upcoming interactions. Ask yourself:

■ How can I let this child know that I see a valuable thing and/or effort in him or her?

- Maybe it would be a direct comment where you let them know that you've "noticed something really cool" about them.

- Maybe it's a gesture where you thank them for showing this side of themselves.

Look (To the Fit of Intervention with the Moment)

Factors that make the intervention of prizing timely and effective:

- Ideally, you're (at least for the moment) letting go of your own agendas. Suspend your focus on "getting" the client to do/learn/change something. Sidestep that inner pull toward making something happen in the moment. Focus instead on tuning in to the effort and want for better things lying "behind" the client's perhaps maladaptive behavior.

- Suspend your own need for kudos. You're the adult and they're the kid. Find your "thank you's" and congratulations elsewhere.

- Trust that the message from you to them (if given enthusiastically and authentically) will resonate even if they don't acknowledge it openly. This is not something they need to be polite about.

- When you're planting seeds via prizing, it doesn't make sense to get mad when it doesn't immediately bear you fruit. Prize with patience.

- Be aware of issues for a particular child, such as trauma reactivity/sensitivity and the need to adjust your words, proximity to the child, use of touch so as to not unduly trigger avoidance, and hyper vigilance.

Leap (Into Action)

Here's what prizing looks like in action:

- Get eye-level, be sincere, and let them know about the "thing" you see in them (e.g., the effort on a math assignment when this is an area that has been challenging due to learning issues or going to recess and trying a game with peers when they have a long history of bullying and peer rejection).

- Ensure that the child will not be put on the spot/socially embarrassed by the input from you. Particularly older child clients will experience the prizing move much differently than you intend if you're putting them on display in front of others, especially peers. At least until your relationship is much stronger with a client, try to focus in on one-on-one, private prizing interactions.

- Keep it brief and speak along these lines . . . "Hey, I just wanted you to know I noticed how you were willing to (insert thing they did/risk they took). I noticed it, think it's awesome, and wanted you to know it matters to me."

- Don't harp on it, and even boil it down to a mere eye-to-eye nod or gesture if you know the child well. Use eye contact and facial expressions that are genuine and responsive to the child—assume an open, engaged, giving mindset.

- Be patient if they don't respond readily. Particularly for kids with low self-esteem, depression, and/or histories of trauma, this positive input might feel discrepant with how they tend to view themselves. They might reject what you're doing or saying altogether. Don't give up! They may be used to people doing so, which only confirms the "script" they've been acting out. Show them with consistent prizing that a new script is possible for them.

- End the interaction with a nod and without an overt or implied demand on your part that the child do or say *anything* in reply. Prizing is a gift. Praise is what often carries an assumption of an in-the-moment response from the child. Let that aspect go.

There's a risk though for clinicians who frequently prize their clients—they might end up looking *forward* to their work even more than in the past. They might find themselves losing track of time and coming to love working with these more challenging kiddos—just for the sake of doing it. Sounds precarious ...

Find ways to prompt yourself, your colleagues, and parents you work with to develop a habit of prizing child clients. Put some sort of visual cue on your desk or somewhere in the room where you'll see it. Make a commitment to find at least one thing with at least one child each day to prize. Watch to see the effect of your efforts. Watch for the ripple effects for the child, others, and for yourself.

The "PRIZE" Model of Mindful Caregiving

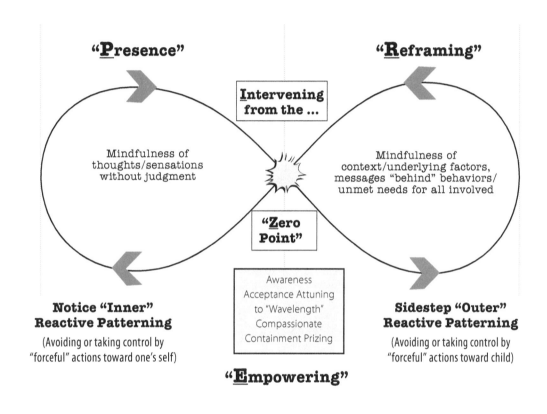

"Presence"

"Reframing"

Intervening
from the ...

Mindfulness of
thoughts/sensations
without judgment

Mindfulness of
context/underlying factors,
messages "behind" behaviors/
unmet needs for all involved

"Zero
Point"

**Notice "Inner"
Reactive Patterning**

(Avoiding or taking control by
"forceful" actions toward one's self)

Awareness
Acceptance Attuning
to "Wavelength"
Compassionate
Containment Prizing

**Sidestep "Outer"
Reactive Patterning**

(Avoiding or taking control by
"forceful" actions toward child)

"Empowering"

Making Peace *IN* the Body

Get Oriented

This is a "body scanning" mindfulness exercise that, with practice, you can do in a matter of a few seconds in order to slow yourself down and relax the body. With practice, you can access this slow scan and its benefits in the midst of challenging meetings, even those with EBD children. Few skills will seem more common sense than this one, and few will elude your awareness when moments are most challenging in your work. This skill requires consistent attention and can, with practice, become routine and rapid to execute; you will claim its soothing benefits.

Listen (To What Actually IS)

Repeat these four steps, stopping for at least a couple of full, slow cycles of breath. Rest your awareness at each body part, feel it fully, and consciously let go of tension there before moving to the next.

Directions

Stop ... Stop what you are doing and soften the muscles of your face.

Lower ... Lower your shoulders and your gaze. Focus on the sensations of your shoulders.

Open ... Open your chest and belly with your breath.

Wilt ... Feel the sensations of your fingertips. Like a plant or flower left out in the sun too long, allow the fingers to "wilt," to go limp.

Continue cycling through and SLOWing these areas of the body. Maintain your concentration on the sensations of each body area as you slowly scan the body, noticing the changes with each pass through with your awareness.

Look (To the Fit of Intervention with the Moment)

This exercise can be a daily companion for checking in with, and letting go of, the tension building up in your body. Whether it's the knot in your stomach during or after a moment of intensity at work with an EBD child client or even the white-knuckled gripping of your steering wheel after being cut off in traffic, you can learn to SLOW and loosen your physical tension.

Look to apply the SLOW scan:

- Just prior to beginning what you anticipate being a difficult session or meeting

- Following such a meeting and before transitioning to the next task/session

- At the end of the day before leaving for home in order to allow the stress of your work to subside from the body

- In the midst of challenging meetings/interactions with others (be they clients or loved ones!)

Leap (Into Action)

What you will likely (and immediately) experience when you try this and other in-the-body mindfulness and stress-reduction practices is that they *do* indeed work. The body often readily responds, eases, and loosens, and we pretty quickly feel better. Try it now for yourself and you'll likely notice this. And yet, why do we rarely keep up with such practices?

The answer? . . . *Habit strength* . . . This practice will stick and grow in its power to slow and ease your rigidity/stress-based tension only if you build it into your *daily* routine. Try linking it (because this particular skill is so brief and do-able even in situations where you're doing other things) to a habit you already have well in hand and do on a daily basis (like starting the engine of your car in the morning or pouring your coffee). Use this daily, mundane activity as a "hitching post" to tie your new SLOWing habit to.

Savoring Breaths

Get Oriented

The following practice can help bolster you for a coming day of difficult work with EBD clients. It can also help you find the "diamond in the rough" of working with these kids—clients who don't often say "thanks"—and where the work is often emotionally charged, aversive, and at times feels as though it's going nowhere.

If we make a practice of looking for (even small) nuggets of positivity in ourselves for showing up to this challenging work, and in our young clients and their families, and if we take these nuggets in and "savor" them, our satisfaction with our work will increase, burnout potential will decrease, and we may even find ourselves and our interventions to be more effective.

Listen (To What Actually IS)

1. Find a comfortable, stable seated position.

2. Bring your attention to the sensations of breathing, feeling the rising of the in-breath and falling of the out-breath for a few moments.

3. Notice how thoughts and emotional body sensations related to challenges of your work show up without you doing anything in particular. Allow these concerns to shift into the background temporarily.

4. Recall an episode in your work that was moving, inspiring, or that mattered deeply in some way.

5. Once the pleasant object is here, keep it in view as you place a hand over your heart. Feel the warmth and the sensation of your heart's beating.

6. As you continue to notice the positive episode or image, begin drawing its positive qualities on the in-breath.

7. Relax into your bodily sensations on the out-breath.

8. Savor the episode and rest in the sensations of the body for 10 full cycles of breath.

9. Return to your stress-laden, to-do thinking if you desire or simply begin with a task at hand with the savored experience still fresh.

Look (To the Fit of Intervention with the Moment)

Don't force this practice of savoring, but also sit through any feelings of resistance, doubt, or "nothing I can think of" and just watch and wait. Something will emerge, even if it's not Grand Canyon–momentous. Don't judge whatever shows up. Just let it be. It could be a funny exchange at the end of a session. A rambunctious kid who finally let you get a word in edgewise. Whatever...

Leap (Into Action)

Consider how this practice leaves you feeling. About your client? About yourself and your work? What is one simple and immediate action you could take that leverages the momentum of the state you're in following this practice? Is there a call you can make that will empower the child, their family, or yourself? Any ideas for how to spark things positively and creatively in an upcoming session or meeting? Are you willing to take that leap now?

Your Personal Mindfulness Laboratory

Get Oriented

If you're invested and willing, building a mindfulness practice for yourself is one of the best ways to end up effectively teaching mindfulness to your child clients. Beyond teaching them these skills directly, your building your own practice will lend credibility and a degree of felt presence that will make ALL of your interventions carry more weight with those you're working with. This requires that you engage in practice activities both inside and outside the office setting, or at home. You'll want to build skills proactively with at-home dedicated practice and with in-session application, especially in moments where application may be useful.

Listen (To What Actually IS)

So, let's explore the basics: mindfulness of breath and senses. It may be helpful to either have a friend read these prompts aloud to you or to make a recording of the instructions with your own voice:

Basic Mindfulness Exercises

1. **Sit with a straight (not rigid) spine either on a cushion or a chair and follow the following prompts:**

    a.) Gently close your eyes and for at least five minutes focus on the sensations of your breathing. Focus your attention on where you feel it most notably (nose, belly, chest).

    b.) If there's any thinking, any mental meandering, come back gently to the awareness of the sensation.

    c.) Simply notice the thoughts as they come and regard them as bubbles that you're reaching out with gentle intention and lightly touching as if with a feather.

d.) Be as curious as possible about each breath as it comes and goes. Notice the gap between inhalation and exhalation. Collect details of every sensation.

e.) Allow your awareness to expand, to go in all directions, to create vast space with each breath.

2. **Again, sit with a straight spine (this facilitates alertness in your system). This time, keep your eyes open (but softly so—without forcing your eyes wide open), and for at least five minutes allow your mind to notice ANY sensation that arises. Follow these prompts:**

   a.) Whatever arises in any of your senses, observe and collect the detail of the sensation. Notice the sounds near and far. Collect the subtleties of movement— digestion, twitching, churning—within your body.

   b.) Notice any soreness or tension and simply let them be as they are. If your mind is drawn into thoughts or some storyline, gently direct your awareness back to whatever is NOW in your awareness.

   c.) Observe each sensation closely. Inspect it without analysis or judgment.

   d.) If you stray into the past or the future, simply note "past" or "future" to yourself and come back to the sensations in the present. How are things changing with the passing seconds? Open and expand into your experience as it shifts (or not) within and around you.

3. **Select a moment when you are able to sit in the vicinity of others without having to actively speak or engage them (think parks and other public areas), and prepare to practice mindful awareness. Sit comfortably and yet upright. Now, do the following:**

   a.) With your eyes closed (if possible, but if not, keep them lightly open), focus your attention on the flow of your breath in and out of your nostrils. Try to focus less on thoughts of breathing and instead focus on noticing the sensations. If your mind wanders, that's fine—just gently come back to the sensation of the breath.

   b.) Shift your focus from your breath and instead focus on any sounds you can notice in your immediate surroundings. What's here? Perhaps the ticking of a clock, air coming through vents, the din of conversations—whatever is nearby. Allow yourself to open up and lean in toward any sound that arises.

   c.) Once you are centered in this "noticing"/"observing" space, gently turn up the "volume" in your imagination to a moderately loud setting (a bit louder than what is actually occurring or if others around you are chatting, just notice that). Continue noticing the sounds as they come. Notice the words and tone of others around you. Focus on the sensations in your body that are prompted by the conversation, the silliness, the fidgeting, the talk from others.

d.) If you find yourself getting caught up in the content of what they are doing, that is fine—gently come back in your awareness to noticing the sensation of experience in your body. Just watch as the words and their impact on your body come and go like passing clouds or like pounding rain that runs down your window, soon to disappear. Notice any thoughts too as they arise and gently observe them, letting them come and go without grabbing onto them. Look for any judgments about others, or even yourself, and just watch them come and go as well. How do you get tangled up in your thoughts? Don't wrestle with them—just see that you've gotten hooked by them and continue to watch them.

e.) Continue listening and noticing for as long as possible. Let the sensations of sound and the ebb and flow of reactions within your body and mind pass through your awareness with as little "ownership" by you as possible.

In particular, what do you notice about your ability to move toward the pressured, less-desirable aspects of what you're observing? What do you notice about the comings and goings of your thoughts, judgments, and reactions? What was difficult? What can you learn about your own tendencies in such situations?

4. **In order to expand this practice, look for ways to create "mindfulness bells" within your daily work routines; mentally designate one or more visible reminders of your intention to become mindful of what is happening for you in the present moment.** It could be whenever your phone rings or when you pour that next cup of coffee. Whatever it is, choose a cue that, unbeknownst to anyone but you, is a prompt for you to take a breath, notice, and collect whatever is in your sense experience, as well as in your thoughts. Observe the contents of the present moment without analysis or judgment. Touch each element with the lightest possible press of your awareness.

Look (To the Fit of Intervention with the Moment)

The goal with these practices is to learn to hold the sensory aspect of your daily emotional experience without the usual, reflexive attempts we all make to change them. This is acceptance of emotion and, again, it is anything but passive and "weak." It requires effort, focus, and a cognitive and emotional resilience shaped by frequent practice.

Consider using these practices (all, if possible) daily for at least 10 minutes—ideally twice a day (for example, first thing in the morning and in the evening before bed). Start with whatever is possible for you, without overburdening yourself. Choose times to practice when there is not much required of you (even if only for a few minutes). The goal of these exercises is to expand your awareness, to take in what's happening moment to moment—to be fully present—thereby enhancing your ability to "hold" what arises in the present moment and respond versus reflexively react.

Yes, you're very busy and, yes, you *do* have time for practicing. The time you spend/waste in reactive mental and emotional states (again, though this *never* happens in working with EBD clients!) is far greater than what you'll invest in the very mindfulness practices that can dramatically reduce this reactivity in the future.

Leap (Into Action)

Once you've practiced for a while, might you consider directly teaching a practice to a client (or group of clients)? Try it out yourself first, and then have a go at teaching the following "grounding" mindfulness practice to kids. Again, the presence you've built via your own practice will immediately translate into conviction and gut-level knowing that will facilitate kids' own internalizations of the skill.

"Redwood Respiration"
Mindfulness of the Breath Practice

The tallest tree in the world (named "Hyperion") is 397.7 feet tall. It is a redwood, an ancient species of tree that can live to be 2,000 years old. Contrary to intuition, their roots actually do not go more than five or six feet into the earth. Instead, they garner their immense stability by shooting roots up to 100 feet away from the trunk.

What follows is a basic breathing practice, anchored in the metaphor of these majestic trees, to help you create stability amid the storms of managing difficult situations with clients.

Directions

- Take in a slow, full breath—down deep into your abdomen.

- Imagine the air continuing down all the way to your feet.

- Exhale fully and then bring in another penetrating, slow breath.

- Imagine the breath again reaching your feet and now feel the sensations of your feet against the floor.

- Take a third breath and imagine the air pushing out your feet, down into the earth, and then quickly traveling far out in every direction underground. You are solid and stable, like an ancient redwood.

- Continue breathing and visualizing this, even while the situation nearby may surge with emotional intensity and harsh conditions. You can, and have, held up through many such storms.

Mindfulness "Roll Call" Routine

(To be practiced outside of the in-the-moment demands in session)

1. Five minutes of mindful focus on the breath. Again, focus your attention on the sensation of breathing, wherever you feel it most notably.

2. Five minutes of mindful noticing of sounds, sensations, and the flow of thought.

3. Ten minutes (or more) of cueing up specific difficult recent episodes or interactions with clients. It may help to have prepared brief notes in advance—perhaps phrases on note cards of what was most taxing, upsetting, frustrating, confusing (insert difficult experience here) regarding your work. Sitting in this centered experience of your body, mind, and surroundings, bring each statement to awareness by glancing at it briefly.

4. And here's the crucial task—notice, observe, and allow whatever arises. That is your task—there's nothing to do in this moment other than hold your experience. Remember, there is space for whatever arises. No matter how displaced you become from a particular reaction, allow yourself to come back to your center through gentle observation of the thoughts, feelings, and sensations.

5. Open your eyes, take a full, deep breath, and immediately take an action with regard to your work around these issues or clients from this centered place. The point here is to experience what it's like to place a call, write a lesson plan, or grade assignments from a place of mindfulness. What do you notice about any changes in the quality of your actions immediately following mindful presence with your experience of recent work? What might happen if you were willing to consistently implement this new habit?

Sitting Meditation Cheat Sheet

What do I do with my posture?

*Sit in a chair or on a cushion in a comfortable, upright "dignified" posture
*Spine straight, but not rigid
*Mouth closed or slightly open, not clenched
*Whole body alert, yet relaxed—comfort is key
*Hands either resting on your thighs or in your lap
*Eyes either lightly open looking downward about four to five feet in front or eyes closed (either is fine.)

What do I do with my attention?

*Focus your awareness on the sensation of the breath wherever you feel it most notably (nostrils, belly, throat)
*Just notice the sensation, perhaps focusing primarily on the out-breath
*Notice the natural pauses or "gaps" in the cycle of your breath
*Don't try to MAKE yourself breathe a certain way; breathe naturally
*Try lightly noting out-breaths by counting them (1–10) to yourself, starting over at one and repeating; the counting is in the "background" with focus mainly on the sensation of breath

What do I do with my thoughts?

*Your mind will chatter/wander with thoughts . . . When you notice it's strayed from breath, simply and GENTLY come back to the sensation of the breath
*Try just noting thoughts as "thoughts" and come back to the breath

What do I do with other sensations?

*Try to simply notice the sensation and come back to the breath; watch the sensation
*If the sensation is powerful, try focusing on IT instead of the breath; how does it change?
*If you are in significant pain/discomfort, try shifting your posture to get more comfortable; don't force anything

***Most importantly . . . Just notice WHAT IS and
LET GO of WHAT SHOULD BE . . .***

Chapter 5

Fostering Authenticity in Communication
with EBD Child and Teen Clients

Authenticity Is the Secret Ingredient

What (It Is)

One of my most important lessons across the many child and teen EBD clients I've worked with as a therapist is that kids usually have good "inauthenticity" radar. Put another way, they are pretty good at detecting BS in those who claim to control their lives—we adults. There are aspects of how the brain functions that make this so, and there are good reasons for us as helpers to consider responding differently when we've messed up. This is true even when the kid is messing up quite a bit themselves. And it's especially true if you're hoping to influence them toward better choices. This lesson came very early in my training as a psychologist.

I was working in a correctional setting for adolescent boys who had committed serious offenses. Basically, it was a prison for boys. One of my young clients was a 16-year-old boy from the worst of neighborhoods. He'd been convicted of selling cocaine, attempted car theft, as well as aggravated assault. He was a "tough" kid. And I was convinced I could crack things open for him—that I could help him own up to what he'd done and truly rehabilitate him—help him so that he no longer hurt others.

"I didn't do a damn thing," he said when asked whether he had done what was clearly spelled out in the black and white of his clinical file. Here was an adolescent who was truly at risk. He needed to admit what he'd done. He needed to learn how not to do these things again. And I was convinced I was the one who could march into the therapy room with him and wrangle him toward change like I had some sort of therapeutic lasso.

I was in my late 20s but, at least in a professional sense, I was an adolescent myself with something to prove. I had to be right, and he needed to help me check off the items on my therapeutic agenda.

The short version of the story is that this young, street-savvy kid broke down in my office during our first session. His girlfriend at home was going to give birth to his baby while he was locked up. He'd miss it and that was digging at him. "I wanna do right by her," he said. He seemed to mean it.

In our second session, I pressed him about his criminal history. "You need to talk about this. Now you have a chance to get this off your chest." I wanted him to take the leap and make himself accountable for his crimes. I wanted to be able to say I got my "thug" client to do so in only

93

two sessions. He sat there silently picking at a hangnail. I was aware of the slow creep of the clock on the wall.

"You talked to me last week about your little baby who's about to be born, right?" I reminded him that he'd told me the week before that his own dad had missed his own birth. I reminded him how much he wanted to "do right" by his own child. I then reminded him of how the judge might decide to postpone his release if he failed to complete treatment in our program. "So, you need to get honest about what you did," I said. "Do you want to get home sooner or later?"

At the time, I was fairly pleased with myself. I thought of myself as Robert Redford's character in the baseball movie *The Natural*. I'd just hit a therapeutic home run into the outfield lights. My supervisor would be impressed.

Instead, I soon needed to slink into my supervisor's office and admit that the boy shut down on me, muttered under his breath for me to "F*** off." I'd made a huge mistake.

I expected a lashing (and deserved it), but instead was given a significant piece of wisdom that I think applies to all of us trying to help kids when they're stuck, particularly when we've played a role in the stuck-ness of things. It comes down to authenticity.

"He had the guts to be real with you," my supervisor said. "So maybe you should think about being real with him."

I learned a lot that day about taking a "one down" position with teenagers, particularly when I've screwed up. Decades of research, and some very recent studies, give significant support to the idea of the importance of owning our mistakes in order to better our credibility and connection with child clients (and their families).

Why (It Matters)

When you authentically apologize, your brain registers it in emotional expressions—contractions of the face (eyes and mouth, in particular) and modifications of aspects of voice (tone, volume). The teen (your observer) is immediately and automatically processing your apology in structures of his or her brain specialized for handling emotional messages—the insula and anterior cingulate cortex, in particular. These areas give the teen a sense of what you're saying emotionally. Other cells, called "mirror neurons," are helping them prepare to respond, perhaps with authenticity themselves.

For many years, research studies in the realm of psychotherapy have shown that the relationship that develops between therapists and clients is the best predictor of how therapy will ultimately turn out. This "alliance" is more powerful than technique, theory, or any other variable in predicting outcomes. And as often happens, therapists make mistakes and "rupture" the relationship with their clients. How effective they are at authentically owning these mistakes has a lot to do with whether the relationship will get back on track. Perhaps it will even, in broken-bone fashion, be stronger than it was before.

When or Where (It Applies)

Kids are looking at us when we screw up. They are paying close attention. Their brains are registering our response, and if we're willing to turn, look them in the eye, and sincerely express our sense of regret, our hope for how the relationship will move forward, then something else happens in the brain: The bond can deepen. Scientists have repeatedly shown the role of the neuromodulator oxytocin in the brain when we're forming connections with each other. When we authentically take a "one down" and apologize instead of debate, lecture, scold, or dismiss an angry, resentful teenager, we might spark oxytocin's release, as opposed to the chemicals of further angst (such as cortisol).

The temptation in moments of tension and conflict with a ramped-up teenager is to follow our brain's lead with flashes of anger (sparked by our neural alarm bell, the amygdala, and informed by our brain's storage of memories of past nasty exchanges). When kids are in our faces or walking away just when we were about to deliver a well-crafted reason for why we did what we did (such as let them down in some way), the pull is for anger-based finger-pointing. We tell ourselves we're "teaching" kids, but really, we're caught up in the torrent of emotion in our brains, and we aren't doing the teen (or our relationship) any good.

How (To Cultivate It)

So, how do we best take a "one down" position in such crossroads moments with our EBD child or teen clients?

- First, review your history with a particular client. How "old" does your pattern of reaction to them feel? What typically happens when you lecture, debate, try to teach, or avoid the issue when they point out that you've dropped the ball or when you've lost control? Take an honest inventory of your reactions. Are you satisfied?

- If you're not, then consider making a commitment to catch yourself. Make it even more solid by letting someone know that you're working on improving your relationship with this particular client (maybe even the kid themselves).

- After you know you've made a significant error, catch and prevent your reaction. Take some space if you need to. Deep breaths, a walk around the block—anything such that you're allowing your emotional surge to subside.

- Return to the client when you're ready or at the next session and ask to talk to them about the last interaction. Tell them they don't need to say or do anything. You just want to let them know something that you've felt badly about. Usually, this will spark a natural sense of curiosity in them. You're already doing a different "dance step" than he or she is used to. They might want to see what will come next.

- Say what feels right, and say it with a direct, honest, respectful attitude. You don't need to gush (and doing so might make a client confused and get in the way of your message). Look them in the eyes and tell them what you did, tell them how it wasn't right, and tell them how you want to fix things for the future. Don't beat yourself up and don't own mistakes that were not yours.

- Steer clear of any temptation to end your admission with a negating "BUT." Don't launch into a laundry list of what they did wrong and how they need to address it. This is not a time for teaching. It's a time for repairing the relationship and for modeling sincerity. That's a *much* more important lesson anyway.

■ Know when to end the conversation. Don't expect anything miraculous. Walk away with them still feeling however they happen to feel. You've planted a seed, and generally, it will take hold. The relationship can grow from moments like this.

This was the case with my tough-guy teen client. I asked him to take a walk with me one day not long after my blunder. We sat on a bench, and I told him he didn't need to say or do anything. "You had the courage to tell me about your baby," I said, "and I tried to use it against you to get you to do something I wanted—that was wrong, and I'm sorry for it."

I think he could tell I meant what I said. I think his brain read the truth of things and sparked a bit of something inside. That something became a therapy relationship where the possibility of healthy change emerged for him.

It may not always turn out this way, but I've witnessed this sort of thing many times. Even if the relationship doesn't rebound in a dramatic way, I like the metaphor of a seed being planted. Kids know when we've had the guts to get real with them.

Sidestep Power Struggles

Get Oriented

As a family therapist, I once worked with a single mom and her 14-year-old son. Despite having a great deal of intellectual ability, this teen had struggled in school for years. The teen's primary obstacles were an angry, irritable mood and attention difficulties; these disrupted his ability to focus as well as to feel competent socially and academically. After weeks of escalating behavior at home (and refusals to leave for school) morphed into months, the mom was desperate.

There would have been a time in my work as a clinician focused on adolescents and their parents that I would have talked to this family about the tug-of-war going on between them. I would have focused on the issues of power and control that led to these outbursts from the teen. I would have worked to give them strategies to meet their control needs in other ways.

However, over the years I've found that, although this approach could be helpful at times, it was only helpful to a point. It missed something. It treated the tug-of-war between parent and teen as if it were a bad thing, a problem to be dropped. What I've learned—and what research increasingly supports—is that when kids and adults struggle most, this tug-of-war needs a different sort of attention. Instead of dropping the tug-of-war rope, parent and teen need to hold on. They need to learn how to keep themselves tethered to one another in healthy ways that get their respective needs met.

This particular boy needed medication and other therapeutic interventions to address underlying attention and emotional issues. However, the relationship between mother and son needed addressing as well—and the problem was not the rope; it was how they were *holding* it. What they needed was a new way of communicating.

Listen (To What Actually IS)
Noticing the Pull Toward Unhelpful Reactivity

The following practice is meant to help you, as well as the caregivers trying to manage the child at home, to identify the specific situational and behavioral triggers that spark unhelpful reactive patterns and, thus, begin a coercive cycle with an EBD child client.

1. Choose a recent conflict-charged situation with the child.

2. In a quiet location, practice a few minutes of mindful breathing, focusing attention on the feeling of the breath in the body.

3. With eyes closed, call to mind the episode with the child. Imagine it in full sensory detail.

4. Notice what's happening in imagination—what is being said, what's done, as well as things like time of day or who else is present.

5. Notice what's happening in terms of thoughts and emotional reactions.

6. Notice any impulses to close up, shut down, avoid, or push back in some way.

7. Open your eyes. Take a few minutes to review the episode and, without rushing to judgment and reacting with labels, see if you can maintain perspective on what was skillful and less-than-skillful in managing the child's behavior.

Look (To the Fit of Intervention with the Moment)

Coach parents and other caregivers to do the following when they find themselves caught in a negative cycle with one of your EBD clients:

1. In the midst of a mild to moderate episode with the child (for safety reasons, don't practice this during the most severe episodes), notice any evidence in your body and thoughts that you are closing in a reactive, rigid, or rapid way. How are you flaring or fleeing or at least experiencing the impulse to?

2. If possible, remove yourself from the situation and sit for a few minutes.

3. Work through steps two through seven from the previous set of steps.

4. Give yourself credit for demonstrating sufficient skill to notice your reactions and interrupt the pattern long enough to work on understanding it more fully!

Continue this sort of data collection across days and weeks, if possible. The more caregivers assume the perspective of a curious observer of their emotional patterning, the more the patterns of interaction with EBD children will shift in a positive direction. Sometimes, just looking helps detangle and loosen things.

Leap (Into Action)

Consider how many years, billions of dollars, and lives were wasted during the nuclear arms race between the United States and the Soviet Union. And now, by contrast, consider the stance that Mahatma Gandhi took with the British Empire. What was different in Gandhi's approach to conflict versus the U.S. approach with the Soviets?

Gandhi acted in the direction of connection, of relationship. He did not look to force separation or leverage violent control. Rather, he sought compassionate, inevitable change. When summarizing his nonviolent philosophy of "satyagraha," Gandhi taught how change amid conflict comes by appealing to the reason and conscience of one's opponent. It is perspective, the ability to assume the healing role—to maintain compassion—that makes this progression toward victory possible.

This is the stance of a responsive leader. As a clinician, you may never approach Gandhi's level of equanimity and perseverance, but you can build a peace-conducive platform for your daily interactions. You can offer compassion, see what's truly behind your EBD clients' anger and acting out, and show respect for their highest self.

So, the next time you're noticing your emotional "rope" being tugged by a client, are you willing to sidestep your impulse to react? Are you willing to let go of reactivity and to actually lead the interaction forward toward possibilities—dare I say, client growth and a shot at professional satisfaction?

Touch the Elephants

Get Oriented

Twenty years of clinical experience with a wide range of challenging client populations—from teen sex offenders to combat veterans to kids at intensive residential and therapeutic school settings. A licensed psychologist who's spoken nationally and internationally, literally having written the book on "mindful management of difficult clients." And I couldn't even start a conversation with my own 6-year-old daughter.

As I gripped the steering wheel and caught glimpses of her as she sat in the back seat, munching away on a bag of stale popcorn, I found myself going stale as well—my courage for breaking open the possible Pandora's box of her pent-up angst over her own behavioral challenges at school was getting the better of me yet again.

I'd spent decades stepping forward into minefields of complex and volatile topics in my clinical work, and my fear of tripping the wires of pain and discomfort for my daughter (and for me) was stopping me short.

When faced with a child or teen you know suffers from an emotional or behavioral condition—or even if their situation is not "diagnosable," yet you're convinced they are struggling in a significant way—then it's important to consider how much you truly want to help them. Is this child's suffering an "elephant in the room" that's blatantly clear and perhaps unaddressed? As a professional helper, ask yourself how much addressing the child's suffering matters to you.

The child's behavior may be off-putting or uncomfortable for you, but it is a "message"—it's their unintentional way of telegraphing their emotional pain. Discomfort and inconvenience to the side, ask yourself with mindful awareness: *When it comes to this child's suffering, am I willing to take the leap of touching the elephant in the room?*

Listen (To What Actually IS)

If you find yourself convinced of your desire to be of help, scan through the following common obstacles to actually doing so. These are the thoughts that may pop up for helpers with EBD clients, effectively scuttling their ability to do so.

Self-Assessment of Caregiver Inner Obstacles to Helping

1. "I'm not good at this stuff; I won't find the right words."

2. "I'm not an expert or trained at this."

3. "I don't want to overstep my boundaries."

4. "I don't want to make a mountain out of a molehill; I don't want to create a problem when one isn't there."

5. "I don't want to spark a huge meltdown."

6. "I don't know what to say."

7. "Somebody else will talk with them, so I don't need to."

8. "They look fine; if something was needed from me, they would tell me."

9. "I tried this once before and it didn't go well."

10. "It's not the right time/place."

11. "I don't have this condition, so who am I to try and help?"

12. "I don't know if this is really necessary in this instance."

If you noted one or more of these thoughts as a common companion when you've been face-to-face with an agitated, upset, disruptive, or withdrawn child, then it's no wonder you've found it challenging to lean into the situation with mindfulness and compassion. Such thinking has a way of stalling the efforts and good intentions of the best of us. It would be completely understandable if you came in toward the kid with either too much "heat" (e.g., trying to force things to change) or not enough "warmth" (e.g., losing track of your heartstrings and bowing out in some way).

Look (To the Fit of Intervention with the Moment)

The act of taking the time to even ask or check up on the child, by itself, helps far more than you will ever realize. Trust yourself. You're doing right here. You're doing good work just thinking about this and the child's needs. Even if you are wrong about the need to help in a particular situation, just the willingness to ask pays so many dividends down the line in the child's life. It plants the seed of compassion exactly when the child needs to believe that their challenges would be heard. It teaches them that such caring is possible, helps them receive compassion, and perhaps spread it to others. They learn to say to themselves something like: "Wow . . . Mr./Ms. X really is trying to get what's happening for me. Maybe, just maybe, they might really care. " In response to such a gift, the child might even venture into believing that they're not as "defective" or "crazy" as they might have assumed. "Maybe I can talk with other adults in the future now and not hide it. Maybe I can even start opening up about stuff."

Mindfulness of our understandable thoughts and sensations in awkward or uncomfortable caregiving situations creates this foundation for compassion and change for kids. It makes possibility possible.

As in the previous list, you might say to yourself, "But I'm not sufficiently trained for this. I'll screw it up. The child will see through me and know I have no idea of what I'm talking about. I'll make it worse."

Expertise or acumen is not what you're trying to prove here anyway. That's not the role you're seeking to achieve. Only the child *themselves* is in charge of how they think and feel, but how you manage yourself—how willing you are to break silence or slow your reactive "get your act together" comments or perspective—determines what ingredients the child will have to work with in a given situation. Your compassionate courage can set the stage for them taking healthy risks and working through their own discomfort. Think of it this way: When you're compassionately and mindfully touching elephants with kids, you're not the "expert" adult; instead, you're just a fellow human being.

So, when a kid is anxious, disruptive, shut down, or says they don't care, the key is for you to lean into your discomfort and do or say something from a stance of mindful awareness that says that you indeed do care. Here's the basic message to the child: *"I want you to know that I am here to help you in any way that I can as your therapist. Believe it or not, I genuinely care."*

Leap (Into Action)

From the back seat, my daughter let me know she didn't want to talk about her troubles at school. "I don't want to talk about it, Daddy!" she yelled. She was quiet for a while, and so was I.

"It makes me embarrassed," she said, quietly, like a small animal venturing out from its safe haven.

We then talked the rest of the way home about how tough such feelings can be, and I had the beautiful experience of listening as she risked walking gingerly over new ground with her budding emotionality. I got to plant a seed and watch in wonder as it sprouted far sooner than I thought possible. I needed only to be willing to bear witness to my own discomfort without flinching. I just needed to lean in.

When you simply *know* a child is in need, and the circumstances seem awkward, make you anxious, or it feels as though it's really better left to others, consider "eyeing the prize" behind the child's behavior by reaching out to the vulnerable part of them that prompted the situation in the first place. This soft spot is truly the "prize," because if you help the child hold it with compassion, incredible things can come of it to expand their life.

Smile at Silence

Get Oriented

What's the one thing that clinicians (being the highly verbal sort that go to graduate school to become therapists) do too much of, particularly when they are nervous, confused, or at a complete loss? You guessed it—talk too much. Although many of us practice so-called "talk therapies," that does not give us a license to over-talk and drown out our clients' own processing of the challenging situations arising in their lives.

EBD clients are especially likely to spark your knee-jerk impulses to talk (often with a question), while waiting and allowing the child to feel their feelings and process your input is much more likely to be effective. These impulses to talk (when they are less than skillful) often come from clinicians' own anxiety/discomfort. It is a crucial skill to learn to NOT speak and let the child client bring their own truth to the table.

Listen (To What Actually IS)

Here's a practice to create more psychological and emotional space for your clients to use for the difficult clinical work you're asking of them:

- The next time to you notice yourself feeling pulled to add another nail to the coffin of your conclusions as to what the client "should" be doing or not doing, or to fill the nervous silence, take in a slow, deep breath into the belly.

- Mentally take inventory of how this moment is manifesting in your bodily sensations. See if you can loosen and ease your tension, letting your body assume a less rigid posture.

Look (To the Fit of Intervention with the Moment)

- Hurry up and "WAIT." In other words, ask yourself:

Why **A**m **I T**alking?

- Let go of any impulse to fill the silence with your conclusions, advice, or attempts to control what happens next. Let that next reminder as to what the client likely already knows (and may feel shame or resentment about) pass, as well as that next question (particularly open-ended ones) that place a high degree of psychological demand on an already taxed client.

Leap (Into Action)

- Wait a second or two longer than feels "natural" to you before you do or say the next thing. It's sometimes in that crucial second or two of delay that I've found many clients to finally come forward with a critical piece of emotional disclosure, expression, or "work" in some fashion. If I'd just launched in because my answer to the "WAIT" question was more about my needs than theirs, I would have squashed this piece of progress from happening.

- Here, the "leaping" is a willingness to forego action. Remember, your emotional presence is the greatest gift to an EBD child client. Just sitting and allowing the silence to happen can send a message to a client that their own experience of things matters— that you respect them enough to hold back from the typical adult tendency to tell them how and what they should think, feel, and do. They likely can feel your impulse to jump in and fill the silence. NOT doing so shows them that in working with you, things can and will be different than they have often experienced with other adults in their lives (and even other past clinicians).

PRACTICE 5.5

Be a (Somewhat) Open Book—
Using Self-Disclosure with Child Clients

Get Oriented

I've told kids and adults I've worked with as a therapist about how I quit playing Little League baseball because of my fear of dropping a fly ball in front of everyone. My story about the time I climbed a mountain in 20 below 0 temperatures with the help of my two good friends is another in-session favorite. I will often answer questions about my preferences: my favorite restaurants, my dislike of those who dare cut me off in traffic. At times, I will share my reactions and feelings with clients young and old. I've gotten angry, and I've even let my eyes well-up and fought the urge to wipe at them.

Though experts in the field differ in opinion, it is my belief that self-disclosure is not inherently bad practice. It is a tool that, well-wielded, can play a powerful role in creating positive change. It can also be a powerful tool for parents.

When done well, a clinician's willingness to reveal themselves helps kids not only learn something to do (or not to do), but it also (and perhaps more importantly) teaches them about authenticity—being direct, honest, and open with others when it matters. In short, clinicians and other caregivers in kids' lives who self-disclose appropriately (and we'll go over the guidelines in a moment) are teaching how to truly connect with others. Let me know if that feels less than important in your work.

Listen (To What Actually IS)

Communication is inevitable between two people who are in each other's presence. To assume you can present a true blank slate to another person (even if it's for a valid, therapeutic reason) is complete fantasy. You can easily prove this for yourself by doing an activity I first experienced during my training.

Sit across from someone, preferably someone you know, but it doesn't really matter. A stranger is fine (and has its own interesting aspects). Make eye contact and hold it. The only direction (other than maintaining your eye-lock with each other) is to *NOT* communicate anything for one minute.

You (and pretty much everyone) doing this will fail. Someone will smile, and the other will at least flinch. One person might sniff, and the other will break eye contact ("Hey, I'm nothing to sniff at! What is she thinking about me?"). Neuroscientists have documented in recent years that our brains are wired for communication, and therefore you *will* react to each other, and whether you intend a message or not, one will be received. And just like in "real" interactions, communication has little to do with intent and everything to do with impact. What people do in response to you is what really matters, regardless of what you wanted.

Look (To the Fit of Intervention with the Moment)

Because self-disclosure is inevitable, instead of avoiding it, clinicians can benefit from the conscious, mindful doling out of sincerity. We hesitate to self-disclose due, ultimately, to fears of failure, censure, or some form of exclusion. As clinicians, we might also fear losing our ground as authority figures with our young clients. Again, we are wired for communication, and that wiring has to do with our innate need for social connection (and, therefore, our avoidance of being shut out in the cold). When our clients are struggling to adapt to change or the demands of life, a well-timed, authentic self-expression, story, anecdote, or even a mere genuine gesture can tip the balance in a positive direction.

What are some examples of times where clinician self-disclosure might be helpful? Consider the following:

- Your 8-year-old client is scared about going to a friend's house for a sleepover for the first time, and you remember a time when you went through something similar.

- A teenager is struggling against peer pressure, and there was a time when you let peer pressure get the best of you.

- You've forgotten to follow through on something very important to your 12-year-old client. You're tempted to give excuses, but you know there were times when adults let you down when you were young.

- Before moving on with the session, you pause to look your child client in the eye and tell them how sincerely "cool" or "awesome" they are for no reason other than it's how you feel and you want them to know it.

Leap (Into Action)

Here are some guidelines to consider in upping the authenticity and injecting self-disclosure into your interactions with EBD child and teen clients.

- **What is the developmental level of the child?** Obviously, teens have the reasoning and comprehension skills to handle more self-disclosure from adults. The key question to ask is whether the self-disclosure will give them a "hook" to hang their experience on. Will it guide and support or will it confuse and make them feel as though you're pressuring them in some way? Are they ready to hear this? *Am I burdening them?*

■ **Is this a "teachable moment?"** If your child client is really upset, often the last thing they want is a lesson, lecture, wag of the finger, or shimmering nugget of advice. Check in with yourself to verify this. Think of a time when you were really upset and someone tried to "teach" you. Did you respond by saying, "Hey, thanks! That's just what I needed"?

■ **Remember that authenticity is the root of connection.** Our social brains know when someone is speaking from the core, and we tend to take note. A well-timed and well-considered story about one's self takes the focus, at least temporarily, off the child. With decreased focus on themselves, there's less distortion, more openness to messages from the outside. They lower their defenses just a bit and helpful messages can get through—even if it's merely a smile and an encouraging word about what their efforts mean to you; how they've impacted you in that moment. When those with less power in an exchange feel the "dominant" one humbling, sharing, giving of their true selves, there is a creative and perhaps curative power there.

■ **Self-disclosure can be disarming during a conflict**. It's hard to argue or take issue with someone else's experience. Kids may not feel your disclosures apply, but they rarely push back and challenge your experience as inherently false. If you're genuine and giving your kid the message that you're not trying to have them feel differently, you're just sharing something about yourself; it can go a long way toward their seeing past the conflict to the connection between you.

■ **Be a good self-disclosure "gambler."** As Kenny Rogers' country song says, you have to know when to hold 'em and when to fold 'em. In therapy, and in relationships with our kids, you need to read your audience and know when you're going too far with self-disclosure. My bottom line as a therapist is to give myself at least five to 10 seconds when the impulse to disclose crosses my mind. During my moment's pause, I ask a simple question, the answer to which determines whether I reveal my inner landscape or keep it well-fenced in: *Whose needs are being met right now? Theirs or mine?*

■ **Keep it "Q and A."** Kids, particularly older ones, don't sign up for interrogations. Get in and get out with what you have to say. Keep it meaningful, genuine, and from sounding anything like a sleep-inducing never-ending story. (That may have worked when they were four, but not anymore.)

We should not deny our child clients access to who we really are. Again, we're communicating our true feelings whether we want to or not. When we're willing to mindfully reveal ourselves to them, we show them how to give their best "presence" to others. What greater lesson is there?

Authenticity Is the Real Secret

Think of a time in your personal life when someone who mattered to you authentically took responsibility and let you know how his or her behavior affected you. Recall how this felt and how it impacted your relationship—your own willingness to engage the person. Comment here:

_____

_____

_____

_____

Now, think of a recent exchange with a difficult child client (or their caregiver) in which you may have pushed or missed the client in some way that may have ruptured the relationship to some degree. Note here what evidence you have that this may have been a rupture. What happened for the client and for you right after you said what you said and did what you did?

_____

_____

_____

_____

Now, ask yourself how you might directly take responsibility for your action with the client. What might you do or say? What might get in the way of doing so? Can you admit your error without placing any expectation on the client? List your reactions here:

_____

_____

_____

_____

How real are you? The following self-assessment activity gives a general sense of your willingness to be authentic, especially when it's tough to do so. This is not an empirically-validated measure with sound psychometrics. It's a brief self-quiz regarding your overall approach to authenticity in relating to others. Think of it as a *Cosmo* quiz with a legitimate purpose. Rate each item as to your general perception of willingness to engage in the action described.

1. When it's clear I've wronged someone, I readily admit it even though it might be embarrassing or lead to other negative consequences to do so.

1	2	3	4	5
Not Willing		Somewhat Willing		Very Willing

2. When I'm feeling something strongly, I tend to express myself despite the opposing views of others whose opinion I value.

1	2	3	4	5
Not Willing		Somewhat Willing		Very Willing

3. I'm clear with others about how I think and feel about them in the moment when these experiences occur for me.

1	2	3	4	5
Not Willing		Somewhat Willing		Very Willing

4. I express *into* people rather than past or through them because it's important for me to have them connect with me around what matters.

1	2	3	4	5
Not Willing		Somewhat Willing		Very Willing

5. When I'm feeling vulnerable, I openly express myself despite the risks.

1	2	3	4	5
Not Willing		Somewhat Willing		Very Willing

6. Despite urges to avoid a difficult interpersonal situation, I do or say what is necessary.

1	2	3	4	5
Not Willing		Somewhat Willing		Very Willing

7. When push comes to shove, I speak from the heart.

1	2	3	4	5
Not Willing		Somewhat Willing		Very Willing

Add your responses to these items. Again, there's no normative sample for comparison, but subjectively, I'd argue that if your total score was 21 or higher, you generally value exhibiting skills indicative of authentic expression.

Consider your score your "authenticity baseline" and return to it later after you've been working for some time to implement the skills and strategies discussed in this chapter (and throughout the book). It will be interesting for you to note any changes in your self-assessment over time.

Clearly, there are times for passionate revelation of one's perspective (even in treatment), and there are certainly times when this is not appropriate (see the following on self-disclosure).

And yet, I'm arguing that authenticity, by and large, is a useful stance for clinicians to assume in managing the trickier interactions in clinical work.

Chapter 6

Skills of Compassionate Containment
of Problem Behavior

PRINCIPLE 6.1

Kids Need Containment
of Their Behavior

What (It Is)

Ask any parent or any staff member in a treatment setting, and they'll give many examples of their EBD kids "testing" them, pushing buttons, and misbehaving in order to get something, avoid something, or just for the heck of it (or so it seems). Homework delay tactics, chore-dodging, tattle-taling, yelling, threatening, and perhaps even more dangerous destructive and aggressive behavior—most caregivers have ridden this merry-go-round of mischief.

As the former clinical director of a therapeutic school for children with emotional and behavioral difficulties, I have directly experienced hundreds of episodes of difficult behavior, and I've come to believe that setting appropriate and compassionate limits on behavior is crucial to children's progress. There seems to be a lot of controversy these days about setting limits or using "behavioral" methods with clients in care settings, particularly clients with trauma or attachment disruption in their clinical profiles. The common view is that consequences such as "time out" or loss of privileges do not teach the skills these children need to address what's driving their misbehavior. Instead, these limits only fuel upset and more problem behavior.

After years of work in this field, I have to admit that I agree with this latter sentiment— limits do not teach new skills. Putting a child in time out or taking away their Xbox system does not teach them how to regulate their anger more effectively, how to appropriately express their embarrassment to a peer, how to ride out anxiety or turn to face fear. Limits do not help the brain "wire up" needed executive function or self-organizational skills.

Why (It Matters)

If limit-setting is out the window, does that mean we should let our clients out the window as well, without regard to what they might do and with no message of accountability for their actions? The problem, in my opinion, is when we throw limit-setting away entirely. Without "fences" around behavior, clients tend not to experience the safety required to settle into the work of building those necessary skills.

A 2003 study points to the likely role that children's "perceived containment" plays into their aggressive behavior.[15] Children perceiving that their caregivers could appropriately "contain" their aggression were less likely to act out than those not picking up this "message" from adults. When limits are not set, particularly for serious, aggressive behavior, messages sent to kids by caregivers (intentionally or not) include:

- *"I don't want to deal with this."*
- *"You cannot be safe."*
- *"You're on your own figuring out how to deal with your feelings."*
- *"People in the real world will get out of your way and bow to your whims and desires."*

Clinicians (and parents, for that matter) must ask themselves what messages they ultimately want their child clients to receive. What do we want kids to learn about how to handle themselves? What do we want them to remember about how we handled ourselves? And here is the nitty-gritty of limit-setting—HOW can it be done in a way that sends the right messages? Without limits, without perceived containment, clients won't slow down enough to take in the teaching caregivers have to offer.

When or Where (It Applies)

"Johnny was power struggling with me. He needed a consequence." I've heard such statements from professional direct care staff members working with EBD child clients many times over the years. I've learned to be quite skeptical and instead of nodding in agreement, begin to dig into things a bit more. What I usually find is a sort of game of tug-of-war between themselves and the child client. These are the situations in care settings where limits can be unhelpful and perhaps destructive, especially for clients (such as those with trauma, attachment, and executive functioning issues) who struggle to manage their relationships with others. It sends them the wrong messages about how difficulty is managed.

Tug-of-war is indeed a silly game: ALL of that straining in order to move a rope a matter of yards. If you've ever played it or watched a match, it is pointless and yet so easily and regularly played. Husbands with wives, co-workers and confidantes, parents with children and, yes, staff members with clients: No one, not even the experienced psychologist writing an article, is above such game playing. What is happening here?

According to psychologist and relationship researcher Dr. John Gottman, when opportunities for connection are missed, relationships fail. When relationships are rife with resentment, attack, and withdrawal (turning "against" or "away"), they fail. Conflict and negative feelings are natural to relationships. It is what is done with these feelings that predict how things turn out. More than anyone else, kids need to learn emotional balance from their caregivers. Children need to watch caregivers manage themselves well and teach them how to do so.

How (To Cultivate It)

The key is to set limits and to do so in a way that is highly attuned to the child's feelings and perspective. Limit-setting is not about becoming an executioner. Caregivers are not to "drop the hammer" on clients. It's not about crushing children under the weight of authority pressure.

Again, these are messages of control and domination, and it suggests the care worker is merely looking to "win" by yanking hard at the rope. Remember, our brains are built for connection, but they are also wired with a lot of emotional "charge." We spark each other, and acting out clients' upset can, at a biological level, be "contagious." Our error is to assume intent (via correspondence bias) and to react with rigid and reactive limits. Yet, limits are not going to teach new skills, and poorly set ones will teach lessons of coercion.

What is needed is limit-setting that flows out of a mindful focus. Caregivers who learn to monitor their own thoughts and emotions—to notice what shows up inside themselves and do so without knee-jerk reaction—can actually respond to a client's difficult behavior. They can avoid "picking up the rope" and can lead the interaction toward something therapeutic. They may indeed set a limit, and it will have the following flavor:

> *"You have a right to be angry AND if you swear in class again, then you won't be able to go outside to play ball for your break."*

In the same sentence that you tell a child that their behavior is inappropriate, crosses the line, and results in a consequence, you can acknowledge the truth and validity of the impulse that spawned it. Feelings and impulses are always acceptable. Bad behavior is not.

The caregiver sets the limit with a full understanding that this child is struggling with feelings of insecurity at being asked to do a math worksheet (he has a learning disability). Although the situation is tense, the staff member is centered within themselves, takes a mindful breath, and speaks slowly, calmly, and seriously to the child. They've walked the child away from other kids (because they're aware of how embarrassed he can get). After setting the limit, they "lead" the child into the practice of a coping strategy (squeezing a squishy ball) while sitting together at the back of the room until things have calmed. This staff member knows to let go of any residue of frustration or anxiety and find a way to let the child know that they've seen their effort to handle the situation.

> *"You're really handling yourself well right now. I'm really looking forward to playing ball with you in a bit."*

Later, the caregiver might be able to talk things through with this child—talk about their feelings about math and how they can work together to fix the situation. They can talk about swearing and how it upsets peers. They can review how much this student cares about his friends in class. They can connect and create a plan for the next time.

Though such a stance may be difficult to maintain, it is indeed the ideal all caregivers should work toward. In treatment organizations, school, and other clinical settings, the administrators charged with supervision and oversight of staff members should work to provide the supports and training to help meet this ideal. Limit-setting should be one of the most frequently reviewed and practiced sets of skills in the toolbox. Limits are set within a human context between client and caregiver, therefore, making them nuanced and challenging. They require the most diligent attention and care to be implemented effectively and therapeutically. Clients need our guidance in order to make progress in treatment. They need us to build fences that are topped more with compassion than anything resembling razor-wire.

In-the-Moment Skills for
Compassionate Containment of Behavior

Get Oriented

Most of us are well aware of the crucial importance of setting appropriate limits on client behavior. Kids with EBD challenges descend into chaos without these boundaries and have a clear perception that they will be monitored and followed up on by adults. If we're not mindful, though, our limits can end up being far more reactive than necessary. They can feel to children much more like "hammers" than the compassionate guiding hands they ideally should be. Here's how to strike the balance between containment and compassion with child clients.

Listen (To What Actually IS)

Before setting a behavioral limit/consequence with an EBD child, begin by doing the following first:

- **GET CALM** ... Check your "presence." Are you mindfully monitoring your bodily senses? You cannot effectively contain behavior if you are doing so reactively and with a high degree of rigidity in your body posture and voice tone. Some of the most powerful and effective limit-setting statements come from a calm, even quiet voice. Volume does not necessarily convey predictability and willingness to follow through. High, harsh volume and rigid body posture DO, however, convey a loss of control and an impulse to regain it by exerting emotional force into the situation. Kids (particularly EBD kids who have experienced/witnessed significant adult instability and violence) are able to perceive that you're emotionally flooded and reactive. They can also sense if you're calm and yet focused and certain in your responses.

- **GET CLEAR INTERNALLY** ... Step up to "understanding." Are you taking a healthy perspective? Are you seeing "behind" the child's behavior to what they are needing? Make sure you're not falling prey to reactive, perceptual biases and that you are clear that kids who are struggling to manage their behavior are doing so because they are protecting themselves (albeit unskillfully). They are not doing so with a master plan of maliciousness and ill will. They are trying to take care of themselves by pushing out at the world that in some way has felt threatening to them.

Look (To the Fit of Intervention with the Moment)

After you have listened to the internal aspects of the moment, before setting the limit out loud to the client, do the following to clarify and target your intervention:

- **GET CLEAR EXTERNALLY** . . . Identify which *specific* behavior is inappropriate (e.g., it can hurt/displace others) as well as how it is "unskillfully" aiming to meet an underlying need (or remove a point of pain or discomfort) for the child.

- **GET CLEAR AS TO PURPOSE** . . . Remember, good limits are done with the client and others (including yourself) in mind. They are meeting the child's needs and not merely your own (in terms of removing the stress of "obnoxious" behavior or "getting rid" of a situation that's blocking you from other things you're trying to do). If it feels as though you're playing emotional tug-of-war with a child, then the limit (or HOW you're setting it) is a bad fit with the moment at hand. Good limit-setting is the building of compassionate fences meant to help create a space inside where children can feel safe and supported in their social and emotional learning.

Leap (Into Action)

Now (finally!), you're ready to state/set the limit with the child. Do the following:

- **GIVE CHOICES** . . . for an appropriate avenue for moving on and meeting needs or of a specific, enforceable consequence that will happen if the behavior continues. Offer to help the child LEARN how to manage the challenge facing them in the moment more skillfully. Offer to do a co-regulation activity to bring things into a feasible emotional space for problem solving.

- **BE REASONABLE** . . . by making sure the limit is focused on helping the child learn the boundary for managing their behavior, not to reactively punish them out of frustration.

- **BE CONSISTENT** . . . by following through—either giving them kudos and caring assistance if they respond appropriately or by following through on the consequence if they do not.

Obviously, these steps need to become second nature in order to be effective. Kids won't give you the time and space to consult this checklist as the situation unfolds (or explodes). Practice these steps both in role-play and discussion with colleagues and teams, as well as in contemplation/ visualization with actual clients. Discuss obstacles and sticking points with colleagues, and elicit their honest feedback as to your strengths and weak points with these skills. No one is perfect at compassionate containment of challenging behavior. You can, however, hone and develop your capacity in this area. Clinicians often are great at fielding the vulnerable, painful feelings of clients. Managing tough behavior can be much more of a challenge. As someone who had a steep learning curve with limit-setting, change IS possible!

A large body of research reveals that people are more likely to do the hard work of changing difficult behaviors when they believe they are choosing to do so.[16] Whether it's addressing addictions, following through on healthy lifestyle choices, or heeding doctor's recommendations, a sense of autonomy is crucial to the change process.

Change is not easy for most of us. For clients with emotional and behavioral challenges, change can be particularly daunting. It's important to empower kids to *choose* the changes their lives require. Pause and think about your own change-resistant behaviors from the past. Perhaps it was smoking, unhealthy eating patterns, or even a nail-biting habit. Did you change when you felt pressured to by others? When you felt down and out? You likely changed only when you felt yourself at the helm, not when you felt pushed from behind.

Real Choices

Let's assume you've set a containing limit on a child's behavior. Now you need to end the interaction with a brief reminder of the child's ability to *choose*:

1. Assuming it is physically safe to say anything further after setting the limit, prepare yourself by softening your demeanor. With a full belly breath, relax your facial expressions and consciously ease the tension in your body.

2. Look at your client. Speaking more softly than when you set the limit, directly state, "What happens next is entirely up to you. You get to decide how you handle this."

3. Check your tone. Be sincere, not sarcastic. Do not, in any way, taunt your client with a "let's see how you handle this" edge.

4. Offer to, assist your client with something that neither diminishes nor negates the consequence you've set. For example, if you've taken away the game or fun activity you had offered for the end of your session, that doesn't mean you can't offer to get the client a glass of water or give well-wishes and pointers for the basketball game coming after school that day. Your willingness to be civil and sincere will help debunk any suspicions that you're rejecting or demeaning them as a person. You "hate" the (bad) behavior, not the kid.

Game It Up!

Get Oriented

Zen master Suzuki Roshi once wrote that "in the beginner's mind there are many options; in the expert's mind there are few." He was underscoring how kids have an inherent curiosity and openness to experience that adults often lose touch with. We are prone to asserting our "knowledge" and "know-how" onto situations that, though often helpful (if not crucial) to solving complex problems, may at times limit our ability to see options and nuances in the moment.

When working with/managing children and teens with EBD, it is understandable and necessary to intervene based on techniques, clarity, and follow-though as to limits and accountability to others for the effects of behavior. We can afford to shift gears at times, particularly when an emotional tug-of-war is on the horizon and sidestep struggle by introducing the principle of "gaming it up" with kids.

If we're willing to catch our negative reactions to EBD kids with mindfulness, we can then reshape the structure of a given moment of interaction with a client with playfulness. "Hey, dude," we can say to the client. "Let's do X right now ... You think you can take me on?" If you lean in with curiosity, energy, and creativity, the frame of a game has the potential to transform an interaction that was teetering toward push-pull with the client and instead help it become a *feeling-felt* and give-and-take. At the same time, you may be teaching a way for the child to more skillfully sidestep emotional and behavioral escalation and regulate themselves more efficiently, you are also intervening in another crucial way—you're offering *attunement* to the child's needs behind their behavior, you're deepening the therapeutic relationship, and you're making it clear the journey forward is a joint endeavor.

Listen (To What Actually IS)

Play and games are much more than mere "wasting time" or "kids being kids." Play is developmental *work*, and it is how kids access skill development interpersonally, emotionally, and cognitively. It is also important for adults as well: Play grounds us in the present moment, opens up options, connects us with others, lowers stress (research supports this), and it helps us manage challenging behavioral situations with EBD clients. In order to leverage "gaming" for this latter function, you first need to recognize that an opportunity to do so has arisen, and then you need to conjure.

Here's a method for learning to listen to the moment at hand and recognize the potential usefulness of a playing/gaming approach. Did you (do you) like "PB & J?"

Making a PB & J with a Child Client

- **P**ause (and drop your adult/expert/control-oriented agenda to get a child to comply or in some fashion do what you want them to do)

- **B**reathe (slowly and deeply, e.g., slow down and shift your physiology)

- **J**ust these thoughts right now ... Just these sensations in my body ... Just these things around me now (notice your thoughts and bodily sensations *just as they are* and notice *what's happening around you* and for your client with curiosity and without judgment—just a few seconds' worth)

Look (To the Fit of Intervention with the Moment)

Now that you've paused and let yourself get curious, you're ready to insert some game-playing into your interaction with the client. Do so, and you may just FREE up the moment and move the interaction toward something more productive.

FREE the Moment

- **F**ind something totally unique, novel, and out of left-field there in the space where you are (e.g., look for a prop or toy or simply remember a paint-myself-in-a-silly-light story from the past. Look for things that are unexpected, nonthreatening, not super competitive and perhaps even about past fun times that the client may be able to connect with).

- **R**elay something funny, interesting, or downright ridiculous about yourself, an object there where you are, or a time in the past when you played, embarrassed yourself, or made an amazing catch at a game.

- **E**ase into simply doing the activity (even if the client doesn't seem into it at first) or asking if the client remembers a similar story, joke, or fun time from the past. Don't react or cajole them if they remain passive or act dismissive of your attempt to engage them. You're *easing* into playfulness—it's a state that can't be forced.

- **E**rase any negativity with enthusiasm and an easy-going, nonthreatening presentation. Don't be over-the-top bubbly or energetic (as this can be off-putting to many EBD kids), but be loose and bring some self-deprecating levity to the moment.

Leap (Into Action)

Leading kids who may be less than playful in a given moment of mild to moderate emotional dysregulation into games takes practice. Kids have an inherent curiosity and desire to connect by way of play. If you show up consistently with "free PB & J," eventually they will bite. You don't have to have an elaborate game or the latest iPad, and you don't have to be a superstar athlete (though it helps if you have a "yeah, I met Tom Brady once" story) to get kids to eventually engage. You simply have to be willing, curious, and consistent. You can make a pencil into a game if you really open your mind (e.g., do that magic trick where you "bend" the pencil by waving it in front of the kid's face or take turns trying to balance the pencil on your nose). You may not have a professional clown's skills for improvisation, but you can certainly get more skillful at gaming it up on the fly if you're willing to make a practice of it. See the handout in Chapter 8 for a handout with some playful game options involving the near-ubiquitous fidget spinners you likely have lying around your office (or perhaps have in your own pocket right now!).

Get "Selfish" with Mindful Self-Care

Get Oriented

As a socially-anxious college student sitting in class, terrified of being called on by my professor, if you'd told me to "gently rest my awareness" on my physical sensation of the fear-sparked knot in my throat, I would have laughed at you. This assumes, of course, I could even squeeze any air out of my anxiety-constricted throat.

As a psychologist, I believe I've lost touch with what I knew in my *own* experience of high levels of emotional distress when I was young. I've benefited from the reminder that, as powerful and helpful as mindfulness-based approaches can be in managing distress, it can legitimately feel (and be) inaccessible to those struggling with bouts of acute stress reactions.

As clinicians, we need to sidestep that inner ogre named "hypocrisy" and do as much attending to our inner worlds as we do to those of our clients. Mindfulness practice is key to this, and yet we need practices that feel accessible when stress (perhaps intense countertransference reactions to an EBD child client) peaks in us. You need a mindfulness foothold to use in the heat of the moment when any meditation cushion is far out of your reach.

Listen (To What Actually IS)

When mountain climbing, it is crucial to anchor your rope as you ascend a sheer rock face—to literally secure yourself as you inch upward with a successive series of stakes or bolts. Those climbing through episodes of intense reactivity to work and life in general need an anchoring structure as well. Instead of setting yourself up for NOT practicing mindful self-care by expecting to practice 30 minutes of mindfulness of the breath or a body scan, it can help to create a series of self-compassionate anchors as you practice, even if it's a stolen moment or two between clients. Such a structure can help create the space for noticing gradual progress and can help minimize the self-berating criticism so common for those whose levels of stress or burnout seem to place longer, more formal meditation practice out of reach.

1. Sit upright in as comfortable a position as possible. Eyes can be open or closed, whichever is more comfortable.

2. Silently begin with a recognition of the reality of stress. Make the words your own, but quietly say something like, "The effects of stress are real in my body and mind right now." Place your attention on the words, and repeat them quietly a few times.

3. Place your attention on a single breath—feel the air coming in, and feel it leave the body.

4. Silently repeat the phrase in step two and consider adding the following: "In paying close attention to this stress in my body; I'm caring for myself."

5. Now try placing your attention on two full cycles of the breath, feeling the sensations of the air coming and going.

6. Add the following self-compassion anchor: "Keeping my focus on how stress feels in my body is not easy, and right now I'm giving myself permission to understand that."

7. Expand the practice out to mindfulness of three to five cycles of breath.

8. Say to yourself: "Though the stress may continue, may my practice and care for myself continue as well."

9. Keep this up a while longer, allowing self-compassion to anchor you as you begin your practice of mindfulness of stress reactions. Let it be a scaffold on which to stand in self-acceptance, and let it help you disarm the inner voice of criticism and failure.

Look (To the Fit of Intervention with the Moment)

Mindfulness practice instructions often suggest for people to place attention on their bodily sensations, to "let go of judgment" and to "rest" or "simply notice" their experiences "just as they are." They often include well-intended nudges that there's "no wrong reaction or experience"—no way to mess up meditation. It's just these sorts of kind sentiments that may make the practice of mindfulness all the more daunting for those whose stress is regularly at fever pitch.

What is one's intention for practicing mindfulness? You can't control or force your way into awareness of stress and at the same time access nonjudgmental awareness regarding uncomfortable sensations you are then experiencing in your body. To the degree there is a pressured goal of "making stress go away," you will be much more likely to criticize yourself as a meditative failure and either write off mindfulness altogether or worse yet, add to a growing sense of self-judgment. It is imperative to approach mindfulness (because mindfulness is too well-established scientifically to dismiss) with a revised perspective, a renewed intention.

Although it's certainly understandable to want to reduce one's suffering, it's important to learn to view mindfulness as a process of gradually opening to experience versus suddenly damming up the flow. Basically, have an intention to be free of the undue suffering that can come with unaddressed stress reactions, but learn to release the *immediate* agenda for making it be the case in every moment of practice.

Leap (Into Action)

Many mindfulness practices could come closer to the reach of those experiencing extremes of stress by imbedding a dollop of self-compassion or self-directed kindness into any meditation practice session. In addition, people need to be helped to ease into more traditional, formal meditation practices; they need help in recognizing the mini-successes along the way. People need much more than the unintended condescension to "just let go"; they need the validation of the urgency their suffering creates for their mindfulness practice, as well as a structure for accessing practices.

Another avenue for taking self-compassionate action with regard to the effects of work-related stress is to actively manage one's physical energy. For centuries in Japan, Shinto practitioners have engaged in a purification ritual called "misogi," which involved dousing oneself in sacred (often very cold) waters. Legend has it that samurai warriors would use this method on occasion to enliven their body and spirit prior to battle. Though I've never traveled to Kyoto to dip myself in the frigid waters of Kiyomizu Temple's "Sound of Wings" waterfall, I have tried a "samurai shower" in my less-than-sacred bathroom at home on occasion.

What I noticed from such a frigid dousing is an immediate shift in my experience of energy in body and mind. And if I'm aware and watching, I also notice how this jolt to my system ripples out and opens me up in the hours that follow. When we do specific, healthy things *and* maintain the mindfulness we've been practicing throughout this book, it's a powerful combination. Particularly when the wilting of energy within our body and mind is on the mild side, it can help to give our systems a nudge toward more energy.

There are no "diets" or "workouts" or five-hour silver energy bullets for neutralizing stress and boosting physical (and mental) energy during our workday. It boils down to a fundamental shift in awareness—a mindset of opening versus closing. When we see ourselves and the world with "open" eyes, we see the unshakeable truth of certain changes to our daily habits around the intake and output of energy.

Energy (including the energy of pain) wants to move freely through our body-mind system. When we pack in so much gunk, it's no wonder energy gets trapped, and we find ourselves prone to serious drain when things become stressful (as can be the case in working with EBD clients!).

And for God's sake, do we all need to move more! The average American sits and watches an average of 19.6 hours of TV per week, and this follows an average of eight hours of sitting at the office per day.[17] Based on the fact that many of us have a natural "slump" due to our hunching over computers and on how the term *text claw* has made its way into the lexicon (it's that ubiquitous smartphone-texting hand posture), it's time for us to put down the screens, stand up, and give energy a chance to move through us.

Our bodies are built for movement, and yet our societal context and years of conditioning call for us to wilt into sofas and video-gaming chairs. Take up Zumba. Walk the dog less for the excretory necessity of doing so and more for your own energetic de-wilting. Stand up from your desk at regular intervals, drop to the carpet, and burpee all over the place! Hurdle-jumping is contagious; worry less about how you look to others, and know that your example will perhaps help others get their energy (what the Chinese traditionally refer to as "qi") flowing as well. Challenge yourself to move throughout the day, break up your sedentary habits, and find yourself stimulated with a steady flow of energy. Cue yourself to mix it up with movement and exercise with reminders on your phone and strategic placement of fitness equipment around your office and home. Make it harder for movement opportunities to recede to the dank corners of your basement or garage.

Use the following practice ideas for giving yourself a good "goosing" in the direction of more proactive management of your energetic self. Do so consistently, and you're doing much to not only manage stress, but to keep your best self in the game of doing challenging work as well.

PINCH Me

With this set of practices, we can remember to experiment with different methods for perking ourselves up. This is more than what you get from an energy drink, however; this is an opportunity to intervene in one's energy system and notice changes that occur from one moment to the next. Instead of a mere jolt, you're also jotting a mental note of what happens to the body-mind when a bit of nudging is applied.

Pull gently (but not too gently!) at your ear lobes. Pinch and hold them for five to 10 seconds, and pay attention to what happens to the sensations there and in other parts of your body when you do so.

Investigate sensations that show up in specific areas of the body as if you're peering into them with the focus and intensity of a powerful microscope. What are the nuances and minute details of each sensation? Give your ear lobes another pinch and pay close attention to the rise, apex, and fall of feeling there. What's happening to your degree of open awareness versus wilting and sluggishness?

Nap! By all means, if it's possible where you are to lean back (or slump forward if you're at a desk) and take a quick nap, DO SO! As we've discussed, this is crucial when driving long distances, but it's also quite helpful to set at timer for 15 or 20 minutes and let your brain do what it needs to do to power up a bit. No shame in doing so, just make sure you're not drooling on that crucial report on your desk!

Chant it up! You don't need to be a monk to reap the benefits of chanting aloud if the situation permits. Without being concerned about hitting the right notes, or saying the "right" or "spiritual" words, try one of the classics like the Tibetan "OM MANI PADME HUNG." What's good about this mantra is that it's conducive to notes that vibrate in your body, which might (particularly if you're paying attention) stimulate your system toward a parting of your mental fog. For stimulation's sake, try chanting words that lead to either inspiration or perspiration (think children, diplomas, mothers-in-law, legal proceedings, and bosses and you'll catch my drift—I'll let you sort these into categories).

Habit-breaking movement. Get up and move about in non-routine ways. Don't stroll in your habitual fashion or stretch in the way you always do. Try "shaking it out" as if your body were a live wire or a puppet being trounced by a hyperactive child holding your strings. Do some burpees or make like you're Bruce Lee around your office.

The obvious point with these "pinch" suggestions is to spark energy into your body-mind. But again, don't just do so blindly. Light the lamp of your attention to these actions as much as you can, so that you bear witness to the changes and brighten your awareness in the process.

Communicate Authentically with Colleagues

Get Oriented

As the old fable goes, an elephant walks into the village of blind folk and, one at a time, people approach this object to identify it by way of touch. One said it was a snake (the trunk); another, a tree (a leg); another, a wall (its broad belly), and all were wrong. Although their experience of touch was totally valid, until they connected with one another and authentically shared what they each had discovered, the full "truth" of the elephant in the room (or town square) could not be known. Here, we make a practice of proactively looking to connect and share with colleagues as we do the difficult work of intervening with EBD children and teens (and their families). Until we truly connect, we're at risk for missing the "elephants" in front of us and perhaps having the weight of it come crashing down on us vis-à-vis burnout.

Listen (To What Actually IS)

Any organic gardener intuitively knows what meditation teacher Thich Nhat Hanh means when he says that you cannot have flowers without garbage. The best flowers grow out of healthy doses of compost—garbage. And compost or garbage is, of course, what all flowers eventually become. Hanh reminds us of what at some level we already know: Bad things can lead to good things, and good things themselves inevitably change.

Pain can become possibility. This is not just a greeting card sentiment, but in order for this to happen, we need to be open to experiencing pain. Empowering change in your interventions requires being aware of the changing tides of pain and a willingness to reach out to others (colleagues and supervisors) for support, perspective, and feedback. Instead of seeing the challenges and frustrations of work with EBD youth as stone solid, can you get curious as to how it has, is, and will certainly always change, perhaps even be grateful for the learning and growth that may come from the harder, sharper edges of the work?

Gratitude Breathing

1. Sitting upright with your eyes closed, call to mind a recent interaction with a client or a colleague that went extremely well, where you connected or shared in something meaningful or fun, or where your interventions or comments really hit home in a helpful way.

2. As the image of this situation appears, notice the sensations in your body.

3. For 10 breaths, sit with that image and any sensations or thoughts that arise.

4. Count each breath gently and silently, keeping your focus on the experience of that good, meaningful time.

5. Open your eyes and notice how you feel. Truly savor this experience for its beauty.

Look (To the Fit of Intervention with the Moment)

Repeat the previous steps. This time, call to mind a recent exchange with this client or colleague that did *not* go well, one that may have involved considerable intensity, challenge, frustration, and perhaps even failure. Notice what arises. Stay with this as you count out 10 breaths. Don't worry about breathing in any particular way, simply notice the breath moving in and out as you focus on the images and sensations from the situation.

Ask yourself: How might the "garbage" of this episode continue to change across ongoing, mindful breaths? More than 10,000 of them? Is there anything you can learn from this situation? How might this challenge or falling short actually be the seed leading eventually to possibility and growth?

And now ask: Who in my professional circle might I share these feelings, thoughts, and insights with? What shows up in my experience now that might pose an obstacle to doing so?

Leap (Into Action)

Pick a colleague and reach out to them. Talk or schedule a time to talk about the "garbage" and seeds of possibility arising in your work with a child client or even in your work with them as a colleague. Notice your hesitations and any anxiety and wonder whether you may be exaggerating and distorting the negative ramifications of any self-disclosure. You will likely find a supportive, even shared, experience with your colleague if you open up and (without gossiping in a negative, blaming way) share with them.

Also, consider the following recommendations in communicating with colleagues in order to facilitate the most supportive and effective context for your work:

"Who, What, Where, When . . ."

■ Do not discuss clients' identifying and clinical information in public settings.

■ Always strive to be mindful of where you are discussing clients so that confidential or sensitive information is not released in a disruptive way. For example, you should not be discussing clients in the elevator or in hallways. *In addition, and very important, avoid having discussions about a client in the presence of other clients.* Even if you're not giving identifying information, *how* you're speaking about another client will have a significant impact on a client who may be listening. And that impact is not likely to be positive.

■ Avoid any sharing (again, even if there are no identifiers) via email. As you may have experienced before, email misses the emotional context required to accurately read others' intentions and is, therefore, prone to miscommunication and distortion. In addition, having any client-related information in emails is a potential liability risk due to its being in writing.

"How . . ."

■ Be vigilant against "gossiping" types of exchanges regarding clients and their families. Avoid any negatively-toned discussions of clients and family members (e.g., "Client X is so _____ and I can't stand how he/she _____ and it is such a pain when he/she _____ and I wish he/she would just wake up and _____ and his/her mom is such a piece of work and I really want to tell her _____"). It is corrosive and burnout-conducive to be "making fun" of clients and their families in private discussions.

■ As we've shown throughout this book, it's crucial to work to maintain a *clinical and compassionate* perspective regarding clients so that, when discussing them, colleagues are less likely to make unhelpful statements. When we allow ourselves to talk negatively and thoughtlessly about clients, we are making it more difficult for ourselves and for those with whom we are sharing our comments to view clients with this balanced perspective; this will negatively impact the work and prime you and your colleagues for more unhelpful reactivity to client problem behavior in the future. Gossip might feel good and connective in the moment, but that connection comes with a high cost: effective work, a supportive work culture, and children in need getting those needs met.

■ Ask yourself during every discussion/conversation about clients whether the content or delivery of your comments would change if the client suddenly walked by or if their parent or another family member were listening. If you notice that you would quickly cut your comments short if such a situation arose, and if you notice that such a mental exercise would curtail a large number of your discussions about clients, then perhaps it would be helpful to reexamine the way in which you discuss clients with others.

- Seek supervision on how to maximize the effectiveness and helpfulness of communication about clients and their families. Be open and solicitous of feedback on how you can improve in this area.

- Be willing to give colleagues direct, and yet compassionate, feedback about interactions with clients and one another. Too often, we avoid giving such feedback for fear of stirring up negativity, tension, or even negative evaluations with supervisors. Basically, we don't want to cause ourselves or others undue pain, and so we keep our feedback to ourselves. We do so at the peril of our clients and the work. Be courageous and willing to touch the "elephants" when colleagues are over-reactive, off-the-mark, burned out, or in some way impeding progress for clients (or for your ability to have a supportive work culture). Lean in and speak the compassionate, yet direct, truth and do so with the following pointers in mind:

  › Be specific (as to the colleague's behavior) versus general (e.g., their character as a person).

  › Describe (the truth of your observations and concerns) versus evaluate (with labeling, judgment, and mere opinion).

  › Focus on the behavior versus the person (this always bears repeating).

  › Maintain the relationship (with compassion and a willingness to own your own part in unhelpful patterns) versus indulge in self-serving behavior (e.g., "getting ahead" or "getting rid" of a colleague).

" . . . and Why."

- Always remember that we are doing very important work with EBD children and teens, and the helpfulness of our communication with each other, with clients, and with their families is crucial to our continued success.

Chapter 7
Using and Teaching Effective Communication Skills

The 3 Cs of
Ironclad Communication

What (It Is)

Consider this quote from an anonymous source: "Your thoughts become your words. Words become your behavior. Behavior becomes your habits. Habits become your values. Values become your destiny." Momentum can grow from the smallest of internal experiences. Untended, our thoughts can evolve into the brightest and darkest aspects of our character. Over time, thoughts coalesce into the emotional inheritances we pass on to child clients who look to us for leadership for building the skills for leading a more connected, flexible daily pattern of living. How we communicate moment-to-moment with EBD clients is crucial to modeling these skills of internal and external flexibility in communication. I call them the "3 Cs." Without adopting these habits in much of our communication with clients (and their family members, as well as other providers/helpers), we run the risk of derailing into reactivity and missed opportunities for progress in treatment.

Why (It Matters)

We pay a high price when we miscommunicate with EBD child clients—particularly when we stray significantly from the "3 Cs." Earlier in this book, we discussed how our brain's anatomy makes anger and reactivity universal, even though these often get in our way. But there's more to the story than just the firing of neurons in the brains of caregivers, clinicians, and kids. Part of what leads everyone involved to feel hopeless and stuck is a pattern of communication that tends to build up over time.

As we also discussed earlier in this book, "coercive cycles" can build up between caregivers and kids through a process of mutual reinforcement and punishment. These coercive cycles are unplanned and yet very destructive and facilitate communication breakdowns between children and adults. It's the *relationship* here—not the child or any power moves, opposition, or manipulation—which is the problem. Either the adult, the child, or both can initiate the cycle, leading to increased disconnection and solidifying the negative pattern.

When we communicate from **connection** with our own thoughts and emotions, **curiosity** as to those happening inside the client, and with **clarity** as to what is required of both you and the client in a given situation, not only will all your interventions be much more effective, but the attachment/alliance with your client will also grow. You will be showing them the way forward toward greater effectiveness in their own messaging of their needs. You will decrease their reliance on maladaptive behavior for roping in adults and peers to notice them. In the end, we all just want to be seen.

When or Where (It Applies)

Emotions tend to *follow* behavior. When we do things, feelings tend to trail along in their wake. Minds, because they are slow on the uptake, fool us into thinking the causal chain goes in the other direction. Depressed people wait for their mood to shift before they will attempt engaging life once again. Anxious folks wait for calm before they step out into the unknown. And overwhelmed, burned-out clinicians wait to feel connection again, to feel at least a flicker of compassion and caring, before they reach out toward their "difficult" EBD clients.

It is especially in situations with the clients you find yourself wanting to push at or away from that it's crucial to lean in toward the task of communicating from a foundation of mindfulness, compassion, and assertive leadership for responsible managing of problems. In moments charged, challenging, or chock full of uncertainty, align with connection, curiosity, and clarity, and your messages will be much more likely to reach the real kid *behind* the maladaptive behavior.

How (To Cultivate It)

In the 3 C's of communication, the goal is not to follow a script, but instead to align with these principles, which ideally follow in sequence. In speaking and acting from each of these, it's important to slow down, breathe, and bring mindfulness and compassion into the interaction, particularly if there's a lot of emotional heat coming from the client (or from you). Safety is, of course, crucial and paramount. Some moments are not moments for direct communication with EBD clients. If the child's frontal lobe is completely offline with rage, it won't matter when you speak from "Cs" or "F-bombs"—little will be processed, and everything verbal will likely only spark more ranting. Again, breathe and bring awareness to the space between you and the client. Go "verbal" only if there's some neuronal breathing room in the client's brain in a given situation. Unless fists or furniture are flying, you likely have a moment to slow down, breathe, and give the 3 Cs a try:

1. **Connect with Your "Truth."** Speak to what's happening then and there in your own thoughts and bodily sensations. For example, "I'm over here noticing myself thinking that things are stuck in this session. I'm thinking how important it is for us to find a way to solve this problem together." Your truth also includes your own feelings, particularly the core, universal emotions of anger/frustration, sadness, fear, confusion, and joy. These feelings include specific surges of sensations in your body. Label them and put them out there (e.g., "I'm definitely noticing a clenching in my stomach and my jaw—this situation is stressful. I think it's my body letting me know that something's important here."). When your thoughts and feelings are happening in the present moment, this is your

indisputable, unarguable "truth." No one can say you're not having them—because you are!

2. **Curiosity as to Other's "Truth."** Follow up a quick accounting of your truth in a given moment with a statement or question coming from a genuine curiosity as to what must be happening that is indisputable and unarguable for your young client in that situation. It might sound like this: "So that's what's happening for me. I'm betting you're thinking and sensing stuff as well right now. If you're up for telling me, I really want to know—doesn't matter what it is."

3. **Clarity as to Needs/Responses/Follow Up.** After waiting and allowing the client to speak to their own experience (their truth), put out there your sense of what YOU and THEY (at least as much as you can tell) need in that situation. Perhaps you need "safety" and "enough calm to be able to work together"; perhaps the client (again, state with curiosity) might need "respect" or "to be understood" or "not reminded of bad, past stuff." It's here that you can ask for specific behaviors from the client (e.g., having a seat, taking a break, lowering voice volume, shifting to less threatening language) and offer some yourself (e.g., "I'll do my best to give you the space to tell me your side of things" or "I can stop starting sentences to you with the words 'you need to.'"). Here, the goal is to be clear about what needs to happen next or what is necessary to get things unstuck. It may also be the time to be clear as to changes, consequences, less-desired events, or situations to come. It's now that we focus on direct, unflinching straight-talk. EBD child clients are all-too-familiar with adults hedging, avoiding, and perhaps outright lying to them. Here, you're being compassionate and yet clear. You're giving them the facts of what is happening or will be happening, and this clarity (even if felt as unpleasant to the child) communicates a respect to the child nonetheless. It basically lets the client know that you think they deserve and can manage the truth of a given situation. These clients need these messages of respect as much as we're courageous enough to muster them.

"Eyeing the Prize" and Truth-Talking with Kids

Get Oriented

Most of us would agree that honesty is not only a good policy, but it's what we most want and need in our relationships with others. In our clinical interactions with challenging-to-work- with (and communicate with) youth, are we willing to tell the "unarguable" truth in order to minimize pain and maximize understanding?

And by this sort of "truth," I'm not talking about some moralistic parting of clouds and downward-shining declarations from on high. I'm not even referring to what most people are focused on when talking about "honesty" in relationships—not lying and casting around blame about the who, what, where, when, and how of our daily doings and mis-doings. No, I'm focused on big "T": The truth that is *always* accurate, can *never* be dismissed or argued away, and is always available—the truth of our present-moment experience—the truth revealed by mindfulness amid the charge of interactions.

We self-protectively "lie" about the deeper, more important truth of what is actually and always the case—what's happening in the only three things we have at our disposal during communication with others: our *bodies* (sensations and emotions), our *thoughts*, and what's most important to us to feel whole, intact, and like our lives are on track (call this our core values or needs).

Learn to speak this truth in the midst of your work, and you'll not only be more effective in your interventions, but you'll also teach truth-talking to the kids most in need of such lessons. Compassionate, mindful communication with kids who are struggling does not mean you're going to be a pushover who lets kids get away with anything. Yes, hold kids accountable for the effects of behavior on others and be willing to do so with a stance of compassion, inner flexibility, and a willingness to focus on THEIR needs, not yours.

Listen (To What Actually IS)

Sit for a moment of silent contemplation and ask yourself:

- Have I ever felt the throb of anger and resentment about a particular child client and told a colleague I was "fine" when asked?

- Have I ever stayed quiet about a client's (or colleague's) choices even though every fiber of my body was screaming out with dread?

- Have I ever snapped, pushed, pulled, or shut down with a young client and said it was something about *them* without saying or doing anything about how I was actually feeling and thinking in that moment?

- Have I ever said "yes" when my strong gut experience was "no" or vice versa?

Few of us tell the "full" truth on anything approaching a consistent basis (authors included)—particularly in interactions where there's a great deal at stake. We hedge, hide, and flail even though we may not be "lying" about the overall and surface-level facts of a given situation.

What follows is a series of mindful "truth-telling" practice steps I use in my work as a psychologist with many clients, especially EBD children.

Look (To the Fit of Intervention with the Moment)

1. Before, during, or right after a difficult interaction with an EBD child client, pause for a moment.

2. Notice sensations of anxiety, discomfort, or frustration that are showing up in your body. Watch them move in your body with curious, compassionate attention. Breathe into and penetrate them. See the "truth" of them—a truth that is direct and undeniable.

3. Silently tighten your left hand into a fist. Draw your attention to the sensations there in your hand—the pulsing and tension. Imagine all the tension, clenching, or surging in your body gravitating to the sensations of your fist.

4. This entire practice may only last a few breaths, but notice how rapidly and readily you can direct your attention to this one area of your body. Breathe into the tension in your hand, regardless of what the other person will/has already said or done. You get to *choose* how you relate to this tension in your body.

5. Now let go of the tension in your left hand. While you're at it, let go and open your right hand as well. Notice the sensations in both hands and the differences and changes as they occur. Watch how you can let go of being "right" and just witness the truth of what both your body and thoughts are saying. There is no need to grab onto or shove at anything; if you're willing, you can just let it all be just as it is: bodily sensations, thoughts passing through your mind.

6. Now with a final, deep breath, ask yourself: *What matters most in this moment? Am I willing to "eye the prize" that matters at this crossroads moment with my client?*

Leap (Into Action)

Intervention that is "**PRIZE**worthy":

1. Establish mindful **Presence** . . . Notice sensations of anxiety, discomfort, or frustration that are showing up in your body as you're about to intervene and let them be just as they are. Breathe into them. Penetrate them with your mindful breathing.

2. **Remember** . . . this client is suffering or stuck in some way and did not choose it (and even if they're doing something negative or disruptive "on purpose" in that moment, they didn't wake up in the morning with a master scheme to mess with everyone).

3. **Intervene** from the "**Zero point**" (e.g., drop all your agendas for meeting your own needs and making yourself comfortable, and focus on what matters most for this child client). INTERVENE by:

   - *Seeing the "truth"* (e.g., specifically stating what you see happening without any labels or judgment—what is the child doing?)

   - *Speaking the truth for* **you** (e.g., saying that you are concerned and want to help, be supportive, listen)

   - *Speaking the truth for* **them** (e.g., saying that you can see that things are "stuck" for them, that you have no way of knowing what it feels like for them, and yet you're curious and willing to listen without judgment or a sense that the client is "bad")

   - *Being the truth* (e.g., actually listen to truly understand the client versus waiting to make your point; also following through on doing things that support, advocate, or give assistance to them; also be a model of flexibility, courage, and compassion with your own behavior as well)

4. **Empower** the client by letting them know you are confident they can manage this, that it's okay to accept help, and that the choice for how they experience and express what's hard for them is always up to them.

Proactive Prompting of
Positive Action

Get Oriented

All kids need nudging from adults from time to time for doing what needs to be done, taking responsibility for the effects of their actions, and for basically behaving like a decent member of the human race. Your EBD child clients need prompting to develop skills of proactive action in a much more urgent sense. Their nervous systems are primed for impulsivity, self-protective shutdowns, and pushing out at others. In your work with these clients, your own skills for teaching (and modeling) proactive self-management are key to their overall progress.

Listen (To What Actually IS)

In order to effectively give a direction to an EBD child to engage a task or respond to a situation at hand, you first need to "listen" with mindfulness as to the accurate and present-moment details of what is happening (in and around you). Even if you only have the span of one full inhale and exhale to do so, try going "IN" (to your thoughts, perceptions, and feelings) before going "OUT" toward the client with a direction, redirection, or prompt for them to do something. Ask yourself:

- WHAT ... are my thoughts and bodily reactions saying?

- WHAT ... is most important to solve/address this situation?

Look (To the Fit of Intervention with the Moment)

Take another breath (yes, you have time for another breath). Hurry up *and wait* in order to create space for effective handling of the situation. Otherwise, you're going to spark a tug-of-war with the client. Now ask yourself:

- WHAT ... specific action from the child is the skillful way for them to manage themselves?

- WHO . . . will have their needs met by my giving a prompt for action (*hint:* It should be more the client's needs than yours)?

- WHERE . . . are we and is this setting the best place to give this prompt? Are people watching/listening? Will the client be embarrassed?

Leap (Into Action)

If you've paused for a moment to ask these questions of yourself and you still have an internal "green light" to prompt the client, take the following steps in order to give the best prompt for the client to do something to manage themselves and the situation more skillfully:

1. Notice and let go of any dismissive furrows on your client's face. Bring mindful presence and continued attention to the needs *behind* your client's behavior.

2. Use a direct, yet positive tone. Maintain eye contact without glaring. If your client is sitting, try sitting or otherwise getting your body at their level before you speak (e.g., don't stand over them).

3. Let go of controlling the outcome. Your only goal is to deliver an effective direction with presence and compassion. The fact that your client may not comply is not your focus. Your focus is on you and effective delivery. Outcomes, in true waterfall fashion, will simply come.

4. Whatever the direction is, make sure you break it down into *clear, specific* steps. Don't simply say, "You need to cut out the attitude"; rather, start with a specific direction such as, "Please lower your volume so that we can hear and understand each other."

5. State the direction *calmly, directly,* and with a *neutral* tone. Don't *ask* your client. This isn't a question. Avoid question phrases like, "Will you . . . ?" or "Might you . . . ?" or "Do you think you could be so kind . . . ?" Research shows that questions often yield noncompliance. An effective prompt is a polite, direct *statement.*

6. Do *not* immediately repeat the prompt. Give your client a moment. If there is no response, repeat the prompt using the same phrasing. Do *not* show frustration or irritation through eye rolling or sighing. This will only escalate into a coercive cycle.

If your client still doesn't respond, simply exit the topic without engaging further. Avoid pleading and nagging, threats, and guilt trips. Hold yourself in presence and know that you've done what you can to model and prompt proactivity and self-management. You may lose this "battle," but the war is won by not fighting it in the first place. Instead, fuel collaboration and harness the child's own stuck-ness and suffering to help them want to move toward new, more proactive and effective self-management patterns of coping.

Elevating Your Emotional Self-Management Philosophy

Get Oriented

Through both direct observation and modeling, caregivers' emotional behaviors and expressiveness influence their children.[18] Though children also learn indirectly from various emotion-eliciting social situations—for example, school, neighborhood, extracurricular activities—parental influence is often viewed as the most significant (Hakim-Larson et al., 2006).[19] This research links the patterns of managing and expressing emotion that children learn from their caregivers to later outcomes, sometimes extending much later into adulthood.

Though your influence on children's inner "philosophy" of how to manage emotions pales in comparison to the impact of your clients' parents, make no mistake that the attachments involved in your clinical work affect kids' inner narratives about what they should (and should not) do with intense emotions when they arise. A great deal is at stake here. There's what happens with your clients' intense emotional experience in the immediate sense, and then there's the patterning they will carry into the future as an emotional heir to the adults who matter to them.

Listen (To What Actually IS)

As clinical director of a therapeutic day school for children with emotional and behavioral issues, I regularly witnessed kids in the midst of volcano-like tantrums or extreme states of agitation. I've seen kids swear, kick, spit, punch, and break everything in sight. I've seen those trying to care for these kids struggle with the emotional impact of their proximity to all this intensity. And then there was me: A guy from a household where anger and volatile emotion were to be avoided at all costs. It depended on the situation, but anger and conflict were definitely taboo. I had developed keen radar for conflict and learned how to sidestep it before anger could spark.

You can imagine the challenges I experienced when I first began a job where conflict was a regular guest in my schedule. When I was paged because a child was in a significant behavioral crisis, screaming, crying, swearing, and yelling, my anxiety would surge, and I would want nothing more than to walk—or run—in the other direction. This avoidance pattern was woefully unworkable.

We're not after insight into the origin of these patterns or scripts here. It doesn't matter much whether mommy or daddy did or didn't do such and such or what this might say about your tendencies toward lollipops or messy desktops. My old pattern of avoidance is not my mom's fault. Indeed, such thinking is not only unhelpful, but it also helps maintain the pattern. Ask yourself, if I learned my unhelpful pattern from my parents, where did *they* learn it? Keep asking, and you'll find there's no one person on the other end of the finger you're pointing.

So, what do we do about these patterns that may facilitate our emotional reactivity in the course of our work? We will only do our best clinical work when we are open and willing to get a full sense of the here-and-now impact of our various patterns, particularly those less than ideal. Our willingness to understand what is happening *now* inside ourselves during interactions with clients (and colleagues) will do much to give clarity and understanding of how our minds are molding the thoughts and emotions we experience in the present moment. This understanding will be the foundation for balanced, well-timed interventions and will be a major factor in preventing ruptures to your therapeutic alliances with clients, as well as buffer you against undue negative stress effects.

Your Style of Managing Negative Emotions

In quiet meditation, ask yourself the following questions. Don't sit analyzing your answers. Instead, gently and without judgment, notice what emerges in your thoughts and emotions as you slowly pose each question. You can pose just a single question for a given period of contemplation or you can pose multiple questions and see how they influence one another. The point here is to cultivate a stance of compassionate *curiosity* as to the patterns that underlie your emotions, particularly the negative emotions sparked by the current situation with your EBD child and teen clients.

- When you are sad or lonely, how do you tend to treat yourself?

- When fear builds inside you, what do you tell yourself about it? What do you feel you need to do?

- When restlessness and anxiety brim, how do you respond?

- When anger either swells inside you or is directed at you, what is your immediate inclination?

- When you are confused and feeling overwhelmed, what does your mind lead you toward? What do you end up doing?

- For any of these emotions, what direction are you pulled—toward them, away from them, or against them?

- Are you able to open to these experiences or do you tend to close in some way? How do you close? How, specifically, might you open?

Look (To the Fit of Intervention with the Moment)

Take a moment and write the following in a journal or on a sheet of paper:

	Open?	Close?
Sadness	_____	_____
Fear	_____	_____
Anger	_____	_____
Anxiety	_____	_____
Confusion	_____	_____

Rate how willing you are to open to or move *into* painful sensations versus how much you tend to close down or move *away* from or *against* such sensations. It's not that you should never close to emotional experiences. Indeed, sometimes, such as in the middle of an immense crisis, it can be helpful to do so in order to address the situation. Here, though, we're interested in your general tendencies toward these emotions. The more closed your patterns are, the more work you'll want to do to create flexibility, so that you can help your clients do so as well.

Leap (Into Action)

Following is an activity I have used on many occasions in the course of conducting family therapy with parents and children struggling with EBD. The intent of this exercise is for you to galvanize your understanding of your own less-than-ideal/skillful emotional patterning from your previous work and place it within the context of work with a specific EBD child or teen client. The goal of this exercise is to place you at the crossroads of "pattern-breaking" action—of doing and saying things (or perhaps just staying silent longer) that serve more skillful and less reactive emotional patterns in the midst of your work with challenging clients.

Sending and Receiving the Real Letter

1. Close your eyes and call your child client to mind. Don't just think about your client though—see him or her vividly in your mind's eye. How do they typically look? How do they sit, walk, and talk? What does your client sound like? No judgments here, just visualize and notice. Once you have them vividly in mind, allow a recent difficult interaction to come to awareness, a time when communication broke down and anger, frustration, or confusion flared. You might imagine it as a movie clip played in slow motion. Again, don't judge, just notice. Don't try to force the memory to surface. Let it come to mind in its own time.

2. Next, proceed through the following steps. You'll need a blank piece of paper and an envelope.

3. Sit in a quiet place where you won't be disturbed for at least 10 to 15 minutes. On the envelope, write the specific external actions—the things you did or said—during this interaction. If you were angry that your client didn't follow through on something important or that they "disrespected" you in some way, write out how you "used a sharp tone" or how you "lectured them on how they've done this before," or that you "looked away and abruptly changed the topic." Whatever your actions were, list them. List them all, even if they include reactions you're now a bit ashamed of, such as scolding or blaming. Write across the front and back of the envelope.

4. Next, taking the blank piece of paper, think about what deeper *message* you wanted your client to receive. What was the intent behind the actions on the envelope? What was the feeling or *need* driving what you said? It might have a lot to do with worry or fear. Perhaps you were deeply concerned for your client's safety. Perhaps (if you're willing to be brutally honest) you were most driven to avoid feeling hopelessly incompetent. You'll likely find that these deeper messages relate to core meanings and needs of yours that have become blocked or stuck in some way. Whatever the deeper message, write out your best sense of these behind-your-behavior intentions and feelings.

5. Fold the letter and slip it into the envelope.

6. Clear your mind. Center yourself with a minute of focusing on your breath. When you are ready, hold the envelope in your hands. Imagine that you are not you anymore—you *are* your client. You have just received this letter in the mail. Read what's written across the envelope—all the actions and words hurled at "you." Read the words slowly and deliberately. To deepen the processing, you can even say them aloud, if you like.

7. Sit for a moment with your eyes closed, feeling whatever arises as you imagine being your client receiving this letter in the mail. What would be your impulse? What would you want to do with this envelope? Notice any thoughts or reactions rising up. It's a safe bet you're noticing little interest in what might be inside the envelope. You might even want to just chuck the whole thing in the trash. Has your client been disregarding *your* letters—the true messages and your core meanings as a clinician trying to help them—because of the emotional and behavioral scrawls all over the envelope?

8. If you were face-to-face with this client in this moment, would your reactions to the same behavior from them change? If you were willing, would you be able to share the real "letter" and rely less on the envelope to state your intentions? What happens to the content, timing, and tenor of your interventions if you act from this space of less reactive patterning—a more inclusive, compassionate, and courageous perspective?

Power Talk

Get Oriented

I n the *Tao Te Ching*, the classic Taoist text from the sixth century, Lao Tzu declares that "the sage acts by doing nothing, teaches without speaking, attends all things without making claim on them." What Lao Tzu refers to here is the ancient Taoist principle of *wu-wei*, the power of change that comes from not trying to force change to happen.

Trees may be firmly rooted to the ground, but they are more flexible and have "give" at the top. There's a *wu-wei* to assuming such a stance. The wind will blow, and yes, it will shove at you. But you won't meet it—your EBD child client's emotions—with rigid resistance. You let the surge of the client's angst push through, and yet you're not going anywhere. Their emotional intensity will not uproot and topple you, as it would that inflexible oak of an old-school grandparent who insists your teen is in need of tough love.

Recent research on the concept of *grit*, or perseverance and emotional commitment to long-term goals, is relevant here. Researchers such as Angela Duckworth at the University of Pennsylvania have presented data showing that students with higher grit scores were significantly more likely to advance in their educations, have higher GPAs, and even rank higher in the National Spelling Bee.[20] Grit was predictive of these outcomes over and above intelligence and other aspects of personality. This unwavering commitment is clearly something we want for our children. It starts with our grit as parents—and here, I mean the willingness and skill to lead your angry teen.

As W. H. Murray wrote in *The Scottish Himalayan Expedition* (1951), "concerning all acts of initiative and creation, there is one elementary truth, the ignorance of which kills countless ideas and splendid plans: that the moment one definitely commits oneself, then providence moves too. A whole stream of events issues from the decision, raising in one's favor all manner of unforeseen incidents, meetings and material assistance." Working with EBD clients requires no less grit than trekking the Himalayas. The results that come from the commitment to practice the skills in this book—despite the discomfort, pain, and outright angst of doing so—opens up possibilities for progress and professional satisfaction that would not otherwise have arisen.

Listen (To What Actually IS)

We all have habits of mind. However, people vary in their inner responses to a situation—there are different ways to process things. Instead of continuing to practice any reactive, self-protective thinking with regard to your EBD clients, how about making a daily practice of inside-out empowerment?

Recent data suggests that self-affirmation statements—such as "this is important to who I am"—can buffer the effects of stress.[21] Here, we'll practice the skill of reconditioning ourselves as helpers toward more adaptive modes of self-talk.

Look (To the Fit of Intervention with the Moment)
Power Question

1. In your journal, write down one of your strengths as a clinician. What is it that you do well, that you truly bring to the work and your clients?

2. Sitting in an upright, aware posture with eyes closed, notice what emerges in you with this question. Don't judge, label, or analyze. Simply witness any inner dialogue or reactions.

3. Next, regardless of any chatter from your inner critic, ask yourself if you are *willing* to act from this place of inner "power."

Leap (Into Action)

1. Do something that exercises and builds on your strengths as a professional. Listen, but don't buy into what your inner critic says to minimize or deflect your strengths. Do something *right now*—no matter how seemingly small—that derives directly from the skill and capacity you bring to your work.

2. Notice how it feels to exercise one of your professional strengths. Notice the effect this has on your thoughts. How might you handle the next situation that arises after having done this? Can you make noticing how it impacts you to perform something well a regular practice?

3. Try doing this activity soon after or in advance of more challenging professional situations. Notice the effect of invoking your power in these tougher times.

It is not arrogance to "toot your own horn"—at least to yourself—about the strengths you manifest in your work. It is highly adaptive and will help you build momentum in your interventions; it will also boost you in times of doubt and "defeat." A habit of practicing power in your self-talk will help you ride out the rough patches. Better yet, it will help you punch right through them.

Ironclad Communication

Professionals Manage Tough Communication by LISTENING . . . LOOKING . . . LEANING IN

Listening . . . (to your thoughts, emotions, and the context of what's happening during a conversation with staff or clients in order to gain perspective and balance)

- LISTEN to your experience (without reacting or "grabbing" at thoughts)
- LISTEN to what seems to be the experience of the other (without judging)
- LISTENING for what's behind my/the other's reactions—what's driving this?
- LISTENING for another perspective other than my own

Looking . . . (for what matters most in this moment)

- LOOKING for what direction is most important for things to go right now
- LOOKING for who needs/doesn't need to be included in solving this situation
- LOOKING at the context and whether this is the right time and place and way to address this

Leaning in . . . (after you've listened to your thoughts and emotions without "following" them, and after looking at the situation, now you can lean in—take action)

- LEAN IN . . . by expressing what you need in this situation
- LEAN IN . . . by asking for the other's help
- LEAN IN . . . by waiting for a less reactive moment to discuss this
- LEAN IN . . . by holding your reactions and NEVER sending reactive messages
- LEAN IN . . . by letting the other know that you're not ok with the current situation and need to address it
- LEAN IN . . . by letting your supervisor know about the situation IF your attempts to address the situation with the other person have not been successful and the problem continues

Ironclad Communication

Tips for Supervisors

Expectations for the Supervisory Relationship

1. How do you ideally want to introduce yourself to a new supervisee?

2. How do you describe your role as a supervisor?

3. How do you set expectations regarding the following aspects of the supervisory relationship?

   - How you work to establish a positive working alliance?

   - How do you/trainee manage conflict?

   - How do you/trainee work together to process awareness of trainee emotions/feelings and self-aspects?

   - How will you/trainee process/address issues of diversity?

   - How is trainee learning style addressed?

   - What is the communication agreement between you?

4. How are expectations set regarding ethics/professional responsibility issues?

   - Boundaries/social interactions between supervisor/trainee and with clients?

   - How will goals for training/supervision be revisited?

   - What will trainees relay to clients regarding your role as supervisor?

   - How do you set expectations regarding confidentiality?

   - How do you discuss/set expectations with trainees regarding your ultimate responsibility for client welfare?

5. What are the expectations regarding conduct of supervisory sessions?

   ■ Structure and content?

   ■ How is session content reviewed?

   ■ What are your expectations for trainee prep prior to supervision meetings?

   ■ What is your style and what are the obstacles for you in giving and receiving feedback?

   ■ How are expectations for feedback loops set with trainees?

   ■ How are you distinguishing formal from informal feedback with trainees?

Structure/Format for Supervision Meetings

1. Overall Performance/Service Delivery

2. Teamwork, Communication, and Collaboration

3. Professional Presentation

4. Documentation and Reporting Responsibilities

5. Supervisee's Interventions

6. Self-Management/Self-Care

Supervision Principles/Values

1. Supervision as a priority in supervisor's activities

2. Availability for consultation and support

3. Collaborative trainee/supervisor relationship

4. Modeling of intervention, communication, and team-building skills

5. Acceptance/tolerance/openness to diversity and multiple perspectives

6. Engagement and involvement as team members

7. Supportive of exploration/growth, yet structuring and directive when indicated

8. Appropriate/professional interpersonal boundaries (not friend, not dictator; self-disclosing, yet with intention)

Ironclad Communication

Clinical Supervision Logistical Checklist
(Tasks to Ensure Trainees Are Completing)

1. Reviewing case record for each person in caseload and formulating initial observations/questions to be addressed
2. Preparing/updating case notes for each person in caseload
3. Attending all scheduled meetings (or making arrangements if need to be absent)
4. Arriving on-time and prepared for classroom and conference meetings
5. Documentation up-to-date and in an acceptable format
6. All out-going letters and reports reviewed and approved by supervisor in advance
7. Reports submitted to supervisors for review AT LEAST 10 DAYS prior to due date
8. Supervisor cc'd on all email communication
9. Checking voice mail/email messages on a daily basis and promptly returning messages
10. Regular presence and assistance on school milieus (e.g., observation of students, assistance in milieu management, consultation/collaboration with classroom teams)
11. Regular/proactive contact with parents/guardians and outside providers (at least bi-weekly for parent contact, phone or in-person)
12. Comes prepared with agenda, questions, concerns to supervision meetings
13. Maintaining up-to-date dissemination of behavioral plans to all relevant staff for students in caseload
14. Proactively addressing any communication issues between teachers/parents/providers
15. Up-to-date information provided to supervisors/relevant team members re: agency services, outside services, and school staff
16. Maintaining up-to-date information for supervisors/relevant team members regarding current status of family functioning for clients
17. Scheduling/organizing service planning/crisis debriefing meetings when indicated
18. Maintaining safeguards re: confidentiality of student information

Chapter 8

Using and Teaching a Proactive Mindset

PRINCIPLE 8.1

The Proactivity Mindset

What (It Is)

Research clearly shows that developing clearer and more consistent problem-solving skills can help kids who struggle with anger to sidestep the ladder of escalation and instead actually address the obstacles that face them.[22]

Anger and emotional agitation make solving problems more difficult, because this reactivity activates brain pathways that make the planning and thinking centers of the prefrontal cerebral cortex less effective. Intense negative emotion narrows people's ability to achieve perspective and facilitates erroneous perceptions (such as the correspondence bias with its blaming tendency that we've already discussed).

Why (It Matters)

You can help EBD child and teen clients manage their emotional volatility by directly modeling, teaching, and guiding them to practice proactive problem-solving skills. With consistent practice—which requires modeling—reactivity can gradually be replaced by an investigatory approach to resolving life dramas. In turn, the success of using such problem-solving skills reinforces the skills. And once kids see how much these skills improve their lives, the skills become self-maintaining.

When or Where (It Applies)

Before you can teach proactive problem-solving to your child clients, you first need to build the skills to catch yourself about to impulsively react to stress and do so yourself. Here are some tips for building this aspect of proactivity into your own daily self-management toolbox. Some of the best teaching comes by way of modeling/observing use of skills, and believe me—your clients are watching!

Doing Despite Discomfort

- Note whether some emotional discomfort is present for you.

- Can you merely *acknowledge* this discomfort? The presence of it?

- What are you willing to do NOW that matters to you and the work despite the discomfort? What options are available to you to address the situation at hand in the present moment? Are you willing to take at least a small action in that direction right now? Stay with your experience of discomfort, touching it with gentle, yet proactive awareness, as if poking each physical sensation of tension, clenching, or pulsing with a nudge from a feather.

- Notice what eventually happens to your ability to engage tasks if you're able to maintain this open, inclusive awareness. What happened to the discomfort?

- How might your willingness to do so despite discomfort impact your ability to get back to satisfaction and self-efficacy in your work?

How (To Cultivate It)

And finally, here are ideas (and a rubric) for bringing proactive problem-solving to bear in the skill sets of the EBD child/teen clients you're working with. Through games and practice-challenge activities (in individual sessions or in groups), coach kids to "SOLVE" problems:

Teach Them to SOLVE Problems

Stop . . . and practice mindfulness to sidestep reactive thoughts and ride out agitation in the body.

Observe . . . what's happening objectively and with a focus on facts rather than judgments or labels.

List . . . all possible solutions—including positive ones and negative ones—you can think of.

Verify . . . what might work by putting an option into action.

Examine . . . the factual results and try another option, if necessary.

And here is a series of very specific steps to use to help younger child clients learn to collaborate with adults in solving problems:

Problem-Solving Procedure for Coaching Proactive Problem-Solving in Child EBD Clients

Use these steps to concretize problem-solving for your child clients and to minimize inadvertent triggering of their self-protective patterns in order to maximize their ability to learn and exhibit these skills in their daily lives.

1. Identify Upset (visual prompting; no adult verbal engagement)

    › "Something is upsetting me"...YES or NO (Client says, points, or checks off box)

2. Clarify Feeling (visual prompting; no adult verbal engagement)

    › "I am feeling ____" (Client either says feeling word or picks from a list)

3. Identify Trigger (visual prompting; no adult verbal engagement)

    › "I am feeling ____ because I'm thinking about ____" (Client says what event, thing, experience is triggering him/her or selects from list)

    › If selecting from list, adult should begin with "domains" (home? school? family? friends? self? past? future?) and move toward specifics

4. "STEP" Up to the Plate (verbal engagement IF behavior/agitation is contained)

    › "Ready to solve the problem?"...YES or NO (Client says, points or checks off box)...If "No" then either wait or begin again at #1

5. Problem SOLVE (adults "turn on" verbal engagement with client as long as she's/he's "engageable")

    › Use the SOLVE rubric presented here

*Reward (or better yet, "prize") the child client if he/she completes the steps and maintains calm/redirects behavior.

The Proactivity Mindset

Sample Self-Regulation "Every-Day-Carry" Plan

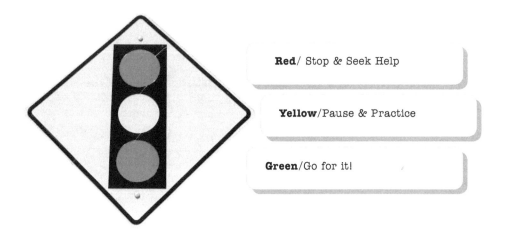

Red/ Stop & Seek Help

Yellow/Pause & Practice

Green/Go for it!

Green... Chunk o' Homework / Do something to organize and get ready / Heaping Helping? / Take a Social Leap / Mini-Meditation / Play a game

Yellow... Willing to "own?" / speak "truth"? / 5 finger breaths/ 3+3=6 / Peekaboo Sgt. Mind!/Safe Place / Where's this stress in 50 years? / SLOW scan

Red... Single deep breath + ask for help / Take a "safety space break" in my room / Remember what happens to ALL waves

Co-Regulation Coaching

Get Oriented

et's back up a bit. Instead of addressing your problem behavior only after it has escalated, what if you (and a client's caregivers) could intervene earlier in the process to shift things toward a calmer state? There's a deer-in-headlights aspect to others' emotional escalations, particularly if you've been there many times before with this particular individual. However, you don't have to passively watch a client build toward full-blown rage.

Listen (To What Actually IS)

The challenge is to use mindfulness to abide with (and assist parents and caregivers in the client's life to abide with) the anxiety, apprehension, and fear you experience and to move toward engaging the client anyway. Then, you can interrupt the angry script and nudge the interaction toward a *co-regulation activity*, a physical or mental activity that calls for mutual give and take.

Before you can coach a child in self-regulation, you first have to realize you have an opportunity to do so. Here's the best way to do so: Notice the felt fact that you're getting a bit edgy, feeling angst, being anxious, or needing to control yourself. Before a client has actually revved past a point of no return, notice your own rising emotional temperature and take that as your cue—obviously, the client's own angst is a cue as well.

The key to making this intervention work is to catch things as early as possible and to use your relationship with the client to lead them into doing a co-regulation activity *with* you. Instead of calling them out for their "problem" verbally and instead of laying out a 30-step plan for intervening to build their coping skills, just walk them into a shared activity that has the potential to either wake them up (if they are shut down and disengaging) or wind them down (if their energy or actions are approaching Tasmanian devil proportions).

Say, "Hey, dude, think fast!" and then (lightly) toss a ball in their direction. Start doing the activity and motion for them to reciprocate or follow suit. Don't give long, wordy preambles; this is the death knell of any co-regulation coaching.

Look (To the Fit of Intervention with the Moment)

Co-regulation work can be as simple as disregarding disrespectful grumbling to toss a ball in your client's direction (with perhaps a quick "heads up!" first). It's a rare kid who will let a ball whack them and bounce off their chest without trying to catch it. You then silently raise your hands in full expectation that the kid will toss—hopefully not hurl—it back to you. The point is to begin a *coordinated cadence*—a flow back and forth between you. This could involve playing catch, spinning a quarter to and fro across the desktop, placing the trash can between you and taking turns to ball newspaper and try to toss it in, playing alley-oop on a basketball court, and doing drop to the floor burpees, for God's sake! The specific activity is less important than the creation of a *resonance*—a cadence—between you, a shared rhythm that pulls your client out of the angry or anxious ruminating and gets their mind and body coordinating with yours. This is co-regulation. It's a skill that requires a combination of playfulness, courage, and timing. These are qualities that, as a clinician of an EBD child or teen, you have undoubtedly demonstrated at some point. Are you willing to call upon them now to teach your client that angry ranting need not be inevitable? Help your client learn that it's possible to break and shake up (perhaps by literally doing so!) the pattern.

Co-regulation activities have double impact: Co-regulation activities physically and mentally disrupt escalation patterns. And co-regulation activities also send teens a clear message of your caring and willing engagement.

Leap (Into Action)

Following are the key steps to any co-regulation activity:

Offering Co-Regulation M & M's

1. Remember to see your client's emotional escalating or vibrating as a *message*, an emotional indicator of a perceived threat or an unmet need.

2. *Move* in support the client. Don't ask, "Hey, would you like to do a co-regulation activity with me like my book suggests?" Instead, just pick up a ball (or whatever prop may be involved) and move toward your client.

3. *Meet* the need. As you toss the ball or engage in some other playful activity that requires a back and forth, express a sincere desire to help your client take care of the inner tension that led to their reactivity in the first place. For example, while tossing a small ball back and forth, you might say, "Hey, I want you to know that I'm not going anywhere. I shifted my schedule so that I could be available to help you with that project. But only if you want my help."

4. *Mold* your client toward self-regulation. As you do the back and forth of the activity, aim for a rhythm—almost as if you're dancing. See if you can slow the cadence of the activity. See if your client can take the lead and set the pace. Let their emotional system get what it needs out of the activity, while still being safe.

5. *Message*, in a brief child- or teen-friendly way, that you really appreciate their effort to downshift the intensity of things in this situation. Say or thumbs-up-gesture that this matters to you and that you respect their willingness to do so. With many EBD child or teen clients, fewer words are more.

Bottom line: Be willing, be creative, be enthusiastic, and be open to showing your own vulnerability. Kids who know you also struggle at times or have weak spots in self-regulation are much more likely to take the risk of learning to shore up their own less-than-skillful self-regulatory habits. Don't just tell them to "calm down" or "choose a coping skill." Show them you're willing to cope right along with them.

Five Mindful Games for Fidget Spinners

1. Meditation Timer Spinner

Focus is focus, whether you're sitting quietly attending to the sensations of your breathing or concentrating on the felt characteristics of a spinner. Take your spinner and put some fun into building focus by doing the following:

- Position your spinner on the tip of an index finger and give it as solid a spin as possible. Really get it going!

- Gently close your eyes.

- Rest your attention on the sensations of your breath.

- Your spinner is now your "meditation timer." Continue focusing on your breathing. Your meditation "micro-session" will end when the spinner comes to a rest on your finger.

- If you get distracted by sounds, other sensations, or even thoughts like "This spin was lame—I can do so much better," don't worry about it—just gently bring your focus back to the feeling of your breath.

- Open your eyes and maybe go for another spin!

2. Engage Your Senses

- Spin again . . . but this time engage the senses. Your mind might race to the past or future, but your senses bring you back to the present.
- Try to focus on what the spinner looks like as it's moving and speeding up or slowing down—or the sound of it spinning and shifting speed. You can also close your eyes and feel the vibration of the spin against your finger or fingers.
- See if you can hear or feel when the spinner slows and stops, not just see when it does. Whichever sense you use for an anchor, keep bringing your mind back to that to strengthen those concentration "muscles" and come back to the present.

3. Spin Out of Autopilot

One fun way to bring more attention to anything we do mindlessly or on autopilot is to try to do things with our non-dominant hand. Explore how the spinning feels different and awkward with your other hand; notice also how and where the senses and the self-talk change when we try to do something more difficult.

4. Spin an Intention

Gaze at your spinner resting on the tip of your finger. Before giving it a good spin, make a kind wish or set an intention (like "less stress before that math test" or "moving on to better things after the breakup") to each "spoke" of your spinner. The wishes can be either for yourself, a friend, or (if you dare) someone who has recently been getting under your skin.

Send the spinner for a whirl and repeat the wishes silently to yourself until it comes to a rest. As the spinner turns, visualize it sending these wishes out into the universe, letting them ripple out in all directions. Afterward, pause and notice how you feel.

5. Dr. Distracto

Play "Dr. Distracto" with a friend and test each other's powers of concentration in a fun way:

- One person begins spinning on one finger.

- The spinner's job is to maintain focus and balance on either the sight, sound, or feel of the spinner REGARDLESS of what the other player—"Dr. Distracto"—does to throw off their focus.

- During the spin, Dr. Distracto will try jokes, goofy voices, animal noises, and more to distract the spinner into dropping the toy. Of course, we'd advise guidelines like no touching or nasty insults. The point is to build focus and have fun, not provoke a fight!

- Take turns as "spinner" and Dr. Distracto until you're thoroughly spun out for now!

These are just some tried and true mindful uses of spinners—I've used these activities with our own kids and therapy clients to good effect.

Getting Out Ahead of Stress

Get Oriented

Ask kids (or adults) to raise their hand if they have never been stressed. If anyone is so snarky as to raise their hand (it happens, particularly with a room full of kids), then tell them you're going to lock them in a laboratory, extract their secret, put it into a bottle, and sell it to make a zillion dollars!—and you will because no one is immune to stress. It's just that some folks are better at relating to it when it shows up. They use tools (like mindfulness, perspective-taking, and problem-solving) to put stress (the thoughts and body reactions that happen in response to challenges in daily life) in its rightful place...the past.

Here are strategies to use with your EBD child clients to help them learn to get more proactive in their relationship to stress—to get on top of it before its weight sits on top of them. The key to helping kids build these coping skills is to have them first realize that the ways in which they've been trying to take care of themselves (and reduce stress) have not been working. Don't tell them they are not working, but instead ask them how "those things are working for them"—let them draw their own conclusions.

Once the client is able to clearly say their approaches are ineffective, and when they can also acknowledge how stress is blocking them from doing the things that matter to them, then they are going to be more likely to engage the following coping skills. Spend whatever time you need with them to get them oriented and willing to take in new possibilities. Jumping into teaching coping skills before you have a willing student is like lecturing to an empty room at best—or a room full of hecklers at worst!

Listen (To What Actually IS)

With a client who is open and available, teach them to grab a "fistful o'mindfulness" when they are feeling the effects of stress:

1. As you likely already do with many child clients, begin by coaching kids to give you "SUDS" ("subjective units of distress") or 0–10 emotion/stress thermometer ratings. Get ratings prior to using any stress reduction strategy or coping skill and then again just

after. Doing so will help them notice in their own direct/felt experience the cause-and-effect impact of their proactive use of stress reduction skills.

2. Have the child scan their body sensations and let you know exactly where in the body they notice the feeling of "stress." Some kids (particularly those with developmental challenges and/or histories of trauma) may require a great deal of practice (and patience on your part) to become attuned to their body sensations. Again, don't force it, and yet don't skip past this step. None of us can put any coping strategies in place if we're not able to notice that tension and distress are showing up in our physical experience. Without being able to get the "message" of upset in our bodies, we keep going in a way that stress and its draining aspect only escalate and build within us. With willingness, a subjective rating, and an inventory of where stress is manifesting, you can proceed to help them learn to take hold of a fistful o'mindfulness! Proceed with the following steps.

3. Sit in an upright, open posture. Lay your hands gently on your thighs, palms up.

4. Take a few deep breaths. Feel your presence and calm in the place you're sitting.

5. When you're ready, close your eyes and focus your attention on the sensations of either your left or right hand. Ball your hand into a fist and hold it as tightly as you can for several seconds. Relax your hand. Repeat this process . . . and again.

6. Notice the difference between the feelings of tension and release.

7. Now, allow your hand to lie open in your lap. Notice the sensations showing up there. Don't just think about your hand. Instead, really sense the pulsing, the tingling, itching—whatever is present in the moment. Continue to notice what you're sensing, whether that's a sensation in the hand or another part of your body—or even a passing thought. Notice how all of these experiences come, go, and change on their own. Recognize that your hand can hold whatever sensations show up. So can you. With mindfulness, when the stress of a moment shows up, you can simply hold it gently. It will come and go on its own.

8. As you repeat this exercise, try saying these phrases out loud or to yourself:

   "Tension will show up as I deal with this—I can choose to let it go."

   "Tough feelings may be there—I can watch them play themselves out until they go away on their own."

   "Stress and bad feelings will probably return—I can always open my palm to them again."

Practice open-hand mindfulness both in moments of calm and tension. Try to remember this activity during challenging interactions at home. No one needs to know as you silently tense and release your fist. Let the tension of the situation release just as the tension in your hand does.

Look (To the Fit of Intervention with the Moment)

Here's another activity to help kids learn to look past their moment of stress to something solid and unmoving—something to help them steady themselves and stay present rather than get whisked away with upset or anger.

When there's a lot happening at home, school, or with friends, it's easy to get overwhelmed. When the mind is unfocused and emotions surge and swirl, we're more likely to say and do things that, without wanting to, make things worse for us (and maybe others, too). In the middle of the chaos of stress, it can be extremely useful to take a few seconds to center and steady your attention. A short balancing and steadying activity can help us find helpful solutions for tough situations.

Motionless Mind

This "to-go" skill works on the same principle as does mastering the spinning teacup ride at an amusement park: Find something in your line of sight that's perfectly still and keep your focus there in order to avoid becoming dizzy and feeling sick. When you're noticing yourself getting mentally tossed about, this skill can help.

1. Scan your situation for something completely and perfectly still—not moving at all. Aim for something that has some heaviness or mass to it—something that's not going anywhere anytime soon.

2. Allow your vision to come to rest on it.

3. In fact, let your mind settle *into* it so that your attention becomes as still and unmoving as that object.

4. Remember that you can always and at any moment choose to bring your attention to as solid and still a place as that object you're looking at. You can choose stability and stillness even when chaos and distraction swirl around you.

5. Stay focused on the object for a few slow, deep breaths, even a few minutes if you can. Challenge someone to see who can stay focused in "motionless mind" the longest!

6. Now let yourself come back to whatever task or "thing" you need to get done. Notice how well you're able to take care if it now versus when you were all whirled about by stress.

Leap (Into Action)

What about when you just can't take it anymore, and it's "too late"—when stress is already getting the best of you? Here's a way to help your clients learn and remember that they can always "walk away from their stressed-out mind" and cut themselves a break. Your EBD clients ideally will learn to give themselves permission to take care of themselves. This requires that they learn to pause and then take action instead of completely shutting down (or lashing out). They ideally learn to allow themselves to go offline for a bit.

Here's the basic message to them: You're not perfect and neither are your skills for managing stress. You can, however, turn this act of walking away itself into a mindfulness and stress management skill. Like the gurus of legend, you can walk the hot coals of the stressful situation you're in.

Walking Away from Your Mind

After taking a break from a stressful situation and as soon as you can, walk to a space where you aren't likely to be disturbed for a few minutes. Better yet, walk outside for a bit. This skill is much more than just taking a walk to cool off. This technique brings your mind back in touch with your body and back in touch with the firm ground around you.

1. Breathe in as you step forward with your right foot.

2. Exhale and slowly place your right foot on the ground; feel the sensations of your foot making contact with the ground.

3. Inhale and slowly lift and step forward with your left foot.

4. Exhale and place your left foot down. Again feel every sensation of the step forward.

5. Continue this slow, steady back and forth of breath and movement. Keep your mind laser-focused on what's happening in the soles of your feet.

6. Right now, realize that, regardless of the speed of movement, you can choose to keep your mind—your attention—grounded. You can test it out by changing the speed of walking or letting go of focusing on your breathing, but keep your mind concentrated on that feeling of contact with the earth.

Do this skill as soon you can after moving away for a break from a really stressful situation, and you'll find yourself returning to your steady, focused mind faster and faster. Do this often enough, and you may find yourself no longer needing to walk away at all.

Self-Care Planning Checklist

Date: _____

Stress Management: Physical Health				
Self-Care Planning Checklist Items	Yes	No	Not Certain	Follow-Up/Action Plan
Adequate sleep on a consistent basis (e.g., feel rested and have sufficient energy and not unreasonable fatigue during the day)				
Diet/eating habits facilitate energy and nutritional needs				
Exercise regularly and have a plan for continuing to build moderate, consistent movement into daily routine				
Leisure activities on a regular and consistent basis				
Adequate breaks during the day				
Work environment supports physical health and well-being				

Stress Management: Physical Health				
Self-Care Planning Checklist Items	**Yes**	**No**	**Not Certain**	**Follow-Up/Action Plan**
Stress Management: Emotional Flexibility				
Self-Care Planning Checklist Items	**Yes**	**No**	**Not Certain**	**Follow-up/Action Plan**
Appropriate "play" with colleagues, clients, and those in my personal life on a regular and consistent basis				
Getting involved in improving the work community without taxing myself				
Clearly identified sources of support in and out of work				
Consistently finding ways to creatively engage work				
Flexibly and "lightly" holding the tough thoughts and experiences that come up in the course of work with clients				
Flexibly and "lightly" holding the tough thoughts and experiences that come up in the course of work with colleagues				
Giving full effort on behalf of clients while letting go of trying to control outcomes for them				

Become a Newbie with Your Work Mind

Get Oriented

The following skill practices help you break free of ingrained ways of viewing your work. The idea here is to see something fresh in the familiar (and perhaps stale) aspects of your daily work life.

Listen (To What Actually IS)

Press Reset

1. Before the start of a session, ask: What am I assuming about this young client?
2. Settle into your seat, aware of bodily sensations and the sensory aspects of being with your client.
3. During the session, notice thoughts … emotional reactions … judgments about the client.
4. Open to what's *new* and might have been missed about the client *or yourself*.

Gap Breathing

When there's a moment of disconnection and stuck-ness with an EBD client, and it feels like the world is at stake, don't just prepare another point you want to make about their behavior and the need for them to change. Instead, use the following steps to connect you to what is most real for your client *behind* the content of whatever is creating the stuck-ness in your interaction. Or, take a moment with your client that is not immensely challenging, but instead rather mundane, and try the following:

1. Turn your attention away from what your client is saying and doing. Instead, focus on their breathing. See if you can notice the rise and fall of their moment-to-moment breath. Start to track the rhythm of their breath. The goal is to tune in to what's happening physically in that moment.

2. Listen through the gaps between your client's words. Notice the small pauses and breaks in speech: the hesitations, the stops and starts, the "ums" and "uhs."

3. Listen to the spaces. Can you hear the moments of meaning in your client's tiny silences?

4. Notice what happens to your own awareness, thoughts, and responses after paying such close attention. How might your next action or intervention be more or less effective than if you'd simply waited and then jumped in with a more typical reaction? You don't need to do or say anything to your client about this, and you need only do it for a few moments.

5. Write down anything you have gleaned about what's most important for the work going forward—from the client's perspective. Return to the RSVP themes: respect, space, validation of feelings, and peers and provisions. Do your client's bodily reactions suggest one of these things is at stake (at least from their perspective)? Do they suggest feelings of hurt, rejection, or failure in some way? Are you willing to get curious about the clues gestures and non-verbal behavior offered?

Look (To the Fit of Intervention with the Moment)
Fresh Eyes

1. Go into the space where you typically work. Pick an object you use daily, the more mundane the better (e.g., think pens, staplers, and maybe even that same plastic fork you've been reusing for the past three months!).

2. Explore this object with your complete attention. See and touch it. Inspect it with curiosity until you move past your mental chatter of judgments and assumptions and notice something *new* about the object.

3. Later, apply the same observational curiosity to your client. Don't poke or sniff them (ill-advised!), but observe them (and your reactions to them) until you notice something you have previously missed. Don't go looking for something negative. Instead, try to notice a detail that communicates something new.

Leap (Into Action)

- Ask yourself: What if I looked with eyes this *fresh* on a regular basis? What if my actions toward this client were informed by this degree of curiosity, these new impressions? What might be different in the work (both in terms of the experience of it, and perhaps in its outcomes)?

- Do something to prompt action based on this new perspective. Place a cue in a visible place to help you "hit reset" and come back into this more open, curious point of view. Set an alert on your phone to remind you to take some other proactive step that will create options and perhaps new intervention possibilities with this client.

PRACTICE 8.5

SNAPPing AWAKE in Challenging Moments

Get Oriented

Challenge is in no short supply in working with kids with emotional and behavioral presentations. How you relate to your own experience of these challenging moments will tee up possibilities for progress in your working these situations through with the client or will further tamp down the child's willingness to work with you (period).

Do the following when the moment at hand is punching you in the gut. Don't just mindlessly tune out or reactively snap; instead, practice SNAPPing awake to awareness, compassion, and therapeutic leadership. When challenge and reactivity arise . . .

Listen (To What Actually IS)

1. **Stop** . . . Pause in what you're doing and give yourself permission to address your reactions.

2. **Notice** . . . sensations in the body and your mind's reactive thoughts. How is the reactivity manifesting in your chest, shoulders, arms, hands, and face? Tune into the flow of your thinking and track it for a moment.

3. **Allow** . . . the thoughts and bodily sensations all to be just as they are. Don't flinch away. Don't try to push them down. Simply choose to watch them.

4. **Penetrate** . . . them all with slow, deep breathing. Take as many of these breaths as you feel you need.

Look (To the Fit of Intervention with the Moment)

5. **Prompt** ... yourself toward compassion for yourself and the client. This is a tough situation, and you are both doing as best you can to manage your discomfort (though there may be more skillful responses each of you could stand to learn!). Know that you'll work to help build more skillful responses to such tough interactions for both the client and yourself for future interactions.

Leap (Into Action)

In order to more skillfully manage moments of your own emotional reactivity with EBD clients, try "snapping AWAKE" to more effective responses. These last steps are a quantum leap forward away from reactivity and failed intervention, and they maximize conditions for kids to open toward learning more adaptive coping skills themselves.

The key lies in the cueing—in remembering and actually following through in the heat of things.

1. **Anticipate** a likely conflict with your teen in the coming days. What marker or signal tends to happen that indicates a blow-up is imminent? This could be your teen's angry glare or your own clenching throat.

2. **Write** down a specific cue that will stand out in the place where you'll be with your teen. For example, this could be an index card with the word "interrupt" written in highlighter. Put the card in a place where you can see it during your work with the client. In your mind, link the object with the marker you identified in the previous step.

3. **(Pre)Arrange** a short but effective strategy you've used previously to calm and take care of yourself (for example, listening to music, taking a bath, working out, going for a walk, drinking a cup of tea).

4. **Keep** to the plan and put it into action during an actual interaction with your client. Do this no matter how much your inner engine churns for further reactivity.

5. Before **Exiting** the interaction, look at your client and say something that acknowledges how valid their feelings are and how valid yours are, as well. Truth is less in the eye of the beholder—it's in the *holder of the feelings as they are felt*. Do not prescribe, recommend, preach, or in any way lecture how your client should be calming down. Let your actions speak (and model it) on their own.

Chapter 9

Finding and
Fueling Purpose

for You and Your Clients

Fueling Purpose by Seeing *Beyond* Behavior

What (It Is)

If there's one thing that is in short supply for children and teens struggling to manage their emotions and behavior, it can be boiled down to a galvanizing sense of purpose—for engaging and fully participating in treatment, digging in as a student, and possibly for their lives more generally. Many of these clients have a hard time seeing much of a future for themselves—at least one that sidesteps a lot of bad stuff. When you've spent a long time (perhaps years) being seen as one and the same with your ("bad") behavior, it's tempting to stop looking down the line: There's nothing beyond your bad-ness and consistent string of failures and losses. EBD clients need their helpers to help them learn to see "beyond"—to identify and cultivate a purpose for the hard work of being a productive, connected human being. To do so, we have to teach these kids to separate themselves from their actions (while maintaining accountability for the negative effects of what they do).

Why (It Matters)

When I was a boy, I loved to toss rocks into the large reservoir down the street from my house. Sometimes I skipped them on the surface. When thin, flat rocks were unavailable, I opted for big chunky ones that would make the biggest *kerplunk!* I loved to stand and watch the water ripple out from the point of impact. As parents, we all hope to trigger such rippling. We hope for a positive impact that will carry forward in our children's lives—and through them into the lives of others we may never meet.

Researchers have documented contagion in moods and behaviors within social networks.[23] Simply by being in a relationship with others, by being associated with others, peoples' likelihood for experiencing significant mood states such as loneliness and depression, as well as problem behaviors such as smoking and overeating, increases dramatically. Moods and behaviors appear to be contagious—or, to put it another way, they can ripple out among people.

The current thinking is that our basic social natures lead us to constantly and automatically process emotional information about the people we encounter. We observe each other's facial expressions, gestures, tones, and emotional tendencies. Without intending to, we subtly mimic one another, sparking emotion and behavior.

We are contagious to the clients we serve—and they to us—whether we intend it or not. Although more research on mood contagion remains to be done, what we know already poses important questions for helpers: What sort of infectious agent do you want to be for your clients? What can you "spread" that will fuel your young clients for years to come? It's here that purpose becomes most important. If we let them see the purpose we derive from working with them, and if we do so authentically and openly, they might just start believing they can care about something beyond their behavior as well.

When or Where (It Applies)

I'm not trying to be flippant here, but I'm going to keep this particular section as brief as possible. When it comes to when or where sparking purpose for EBD clients applies, I suggest the following:

- *Always*
- *In every situation*

How (To Cultivate It)

So, if you're sold that helping your clients derive purpose is important for your work, here's the key way to do so: by drilling down to your own and bringing it to the surface. Here are some ways to do so:

Ask yourself: What's HARD for you in doing/thinking about doing this work with EBD child and teen clients? Don't think too much . . . what jumps to mind? What are the tough-to-swallow aspects? What are you *not* looking forward to? Try writing out your thoughts in a journal.

As I said earlier, I liked skipping rocks on ponds and lakes as a kid. Close your eyes and visualize your own "pebble" meditation.

Imagine tossing a small rock into a large, deep lake. With your mind's eye, follow the rock down through the water. As it falls gently downward into the deepest corner of the lake, ask yourself, "Why did I show up to work with these kids? What am I aiming for in working with them? What matters about what I do?"

Listen with patient awareness for answers to rise up from those deep recesses of the lake. Allow your attention to drop down with the rock into the deepest aspects of your heart and mind. What emerges there?

While in this calm, centered space, see yourself sitting across from one of your young clients (it doesn't really matter who—let your mind gravitate toward someone). What might this kid say to you (if they could) about what it is that you do, or at least intend to do, that really matters to them. Think less of what you want to accomplish in your work with this client and more of the direction you want the work to be heading, like a point on a compass. What would you have them say? Be as specific as possible. That client is now telling you what they will always remember about your work for years to come. What, like a rock hitting the water, will you do in your work that will ripple out and transform others in ways planned and less so?

And now, open your eyes. Touch a forefinger to the thumb of one of your hands as you think about this visualization and what emerged in thought and your feelings. Do you think you'll remember what's most meaningful right now (e.g., your purpose for your work) if I walk up to you and silently hold up my own hand and make the same finger-to-thumb gesture? Do you think you'd be able to conjure what mattered to you about your work—a week from now ... a month from now ... the end of your career?

This is your purpose ... it's down in your deepest waters. The thing is, it's there for your clients as well. Unfortunately, the storms on the surface of things may be stirring their waters, muddying and clouding their view down to the bottom. You'll need to show them examples of your passion, your purpose, and hang in despite their disavowals that you're "really in it for them" or that it's more than "just your job" or a "just your paycheck."

If you help them hang in long enough to believe in your purpose for your work with them, perhaps the water will go sufficiently still for them to slowly start seeing into their own depths; their own reasons for moving, doing, and ultimately risking will emerge into view.

When they do, and in order to help usher them toward the surface, keep it clear that you see a vast difference between the storm of their emotions and behavior on the surface (e.g., their behavioral challenges) and instead you think the "real deal" of who they are is down deep where the water is always still. Help them believe that you're not only interested in knowing what's there (e.g., their true selves), but that you also *know* with certainty that these depths have worth and something to offer the world.

Let 'em Rise to the Challenge

Get Oriented

I got some skeptical looks from colleagues. "Really?" one asked. "You're going to take *those* kids and put a nail gun in their hands?" My friend was referring to how I'd signed myself and a small group of teen boys from the residential program I worked for at the time to go on a Saturday morning for an all-day build for Habitat for Humanity. Some of these kids had really significant aggressive and dangerous behavior in their not-so-distant histories. I began to wonder to myself whether I'd made a mistake.

Though no one ended up with a nail gun to hold that Saturday, there were plenty of opportunities for these "acting out" youth to take advantage of the relative laxness and leeway of the situation. Yet not a single one of them did. Not only that, but they also worked hard in the 90-degree heat for hours on end, painting the interior of this young family's future home.

Then there was the moment when I caught sight of the father of that family speaking alone to one of the boys from our program (a boy with a particularly egregious history of volatile and extreme behavior). "I just want you to know something," said the man who would own his first home thanks to the generosity of Habitat for Humanity. The boy looked at him intently. "You are doing something amazing today," the man said, a bit choked up with emotion. "You're helping me provide a home for my family, and I can never thank you enough." The boy said nothing, but simply nodded at the father as he held a paint roller in one hand, his other covered with blotches of eggshell enamel.

I've seen this sort of thing happen time and again in my work with at-risk youth. If they are given the opportunity and vehicle, they will often rise up to a challenge. The parts of them that want to be whole—that want to do something worthy of respect—these parts nudge them onward and upward.

Listen (To What Actually IS)

As clinicians and helpers, we often bide our time and wait for our young clients to show us they are "ready" (via safe, stable, blemish-free behavior) to have the *privilege* of having access to various opportunities. What if the kids are waiting as well . . . waiting for us to lead them away from their reactivity and poor self-esteem that we're silently yet powerfully messaging to them with our basic message that they're not yet "ready"? Children have no choice but to be the heirs of adults' expectations. Sure, we need to take safety into consideration. Absolutely, we must attend to following through on limits/consequences previously set in response to acting-out behavior. Eventually, though, as caregivers, we will have to consider what inheritance of expectation and worth will go to the kids we're charged with supporting.

What if we were willing to listen more "lightly" to our doubting, delaying minds and instead move in the direction of offering kids opportunities to show (and feel) worth. Would they notice the change, the shift in our expectations? What message might that send?

Try the following practice to get your mind out of any ruts of unnecessary hypervigilant naysaying with regard to offering these EBD clients chances to assume responsibilities, give to others, and contribute or take charge in some way. Are we willing to be more than the story we tell ourselves?

More Than Our Stories

1. With a journal or a sheet of paper in hand, set a timer for one minute. As rapidly as possible, list as many positive attributes or qualities about a specific EBD client that you can.

2. Set your timer for another minute. Do the same for their negative qualities—their behaviors and patterns of reaction. Again, write them down as quickly as you can.

3. Close your eyes and take a few centering breaths; perhaps practice mindful breathing.

4. Open your eyes. Survey both lists. These lists basically summarize the "story" you tell yourself about this client. Notice how it feels to read your story. Is your story the most accurate piece of nonfiction ever written? Is there no room for considering that your mind may be fixating on at least a small aspect of fiction when it comes to what this child "will" do in the future if put in a position of access to shenanigans?

5. Ask yourself: Is this story sufficient? Does it fully describe every possible angle on this client and the situation at hand? Are there things left unaccounted for here?

Look (To the Fit of Intervention with the Moment)
Learned Hopefulness

Let's end by visiting a well-researched principle of positive psychology. Psychologist Carol Dweck has shown that the *mindset* we adopt when facing obstacles determines whether we believe that we can learn and grow or we believe that outcomes are set in stone by uncontrollable external factors.[24] We approach life with either a *growth* or a *fixed* mindset. This mindset impacts our willingness and capacity for change. It certainly affects clinicians' perspectives and willingness to craft creative options for behavior-challenged kids to rise up into responsibility and competency. Further, Dweck's research points to how our children's mindset is strongly influenced by our own. Children are the heirs not only of our actions, but of our mindsets as well.

In a journal, contemplate how:

- You will continue to develop yourself as a clinician—that you are still changing and growing, regardless of your stage of career or years of experience.

- The challenges you and your clients face are opportunities for growth—that we might consider creating challenges versus simply training kids to "reduce stress," "manage emotions," and "self-regulate" in response to them.

- You can sidestep judgments and often avert escalation episodes; stop avoiding the very aspects of your situations of challenge, community, and contribution that, if you leaned into them, might open up possibilities for "challenged" kids to rise.

Leap (Into Action)

The next time you walk into the room with a client with whom you've held a naysaying story of negative expectations, set an intention for the fresh possibilities that the coming moments will bring. Setting this intention—and being willing to do so over and over again despite the unskillful actions the client may engage in—will nudge the child forward toward the risk required for truly rising to meet new, higher standards for their actions in daily life.

Foster Belonging

Get Oriented

Clinicians working with EBD clients manage sessions effectively when they think beyond (and "behind") the behavior of these young people. It's easy for clinicians to chase individual behaviors and miss opportunities for managing and truly leading the moment.

EBD clients typically have long histories of failure in the home, school, and in prior clinical settings. Therapy can be very intimidating. They need clinicians who can shepherd them toward a clear sense of community (in all the settings of their daily life) where they begin to believe they belong to something greater than themselves.

Listen (To What Actually IS)

EBD children often experience significant stigma for their learning and mental health difficulties, as well as their histories of school failure. They need their caregivers to help them restore their self-efficacy and worth as students, individuals, and contributing members of groups. Those working with these clients should endeavor to help them believe that they matter and belong *no matter what.*

Before you can shift an EBD child client in the direction of belonging, you first have to focus on helping them *feel felt* for the pain of their histories leading them toward negative self-perceptions and perhaps a long list of unskillful actions. As a supervisor of mine said many years ago, you can't make a client move from point A to point B—you can only stand with them at A, and then once they realize you are firmly planted next to them, they MIGHT be willing to allow you to walk with them toward B. Kids who do not believe they deserve to belong to groups, schools, or even relationships with caring clinicians will sometimes outright push back at attempts to link them up with needed supports, nice people, sports teams, or even their favorite fun activities if their prevailing feeling is unworthiness.

Resist the impulse to yank the client toward a belongingness support (even if it is a no-brainer and you KNOW the kiddo will benefit and like it). Know that the client can feel your desire to link them with positive supports and will resist. Instead, rest your impulse (and practice mindfulness as discussed in this book). Breathe into and through it, and instead let the client know that it will be up to them to make the choice to engage this support. Underscoring their autonomy empowers clients for actually being more likely to move toward these choices.

Look (To the Fit of Intervention with the Moment)

Call to mind a specific client. Cue up specific reminders of this child (e.g., use multiple senses) and visualize specific situations in which this child MIGHT have/will benefit from belonging to certain groups, activities, or relationships. Get this child and some sample situations so vivid in your mind's eye that you can conjure a bit of that impulse to "get them" connected—belonging—to something that will matter. Breathe into and through the impulse and let it pass. Say and/or do things in your imagination that let the child know that you get that they have felt "stuck" or "frustrated" with past schools, events, activities, and relationships.

Hover in this accepting, patient internal space until it feels "organic" (e.g., natural) that the child seems interested in possibilities for belonging. Look for signs (even if very faint) of them entertaining the idea of connection with things outside their negative frame of self-reference. Look for evidence in terms of their asking questions about these belongingness possibilities, even if there's still an overt "not me"/dismissive tone. Continue hovering inside yourself with patience, and yet gently be willing to make them an OFFER to help them get connected.

An "offer" is an invitation to belongingness. It's a series of simple steps for helping them move from A (amotivation and disconnection) to B (belongingness). Here are the steps of a solid OFFER:

1. **Observe** . . . How they are already thinking and feeling about past things to which they belonged (and perhaps failed at or were in some way excluded). Let them know that whatever they are thinking and feeling about these things makes complete sense to you. HANG OUT here longer than would be your preference.

2. **Frame** . . . (e.g., put a "frame" around) the likes, desires, skills, and ideas the client ALREADY accepts about themselves and, to some degree, values. You're underscoring and emphasizing the things they already see about themselves (including skills they possess) that in some way (even if it's a small stretch) would be germane to the belongingness activity or activities available (or that you have in mind). Continue to resist the urge to nudge them toward the belongingness item/event. You're aiming to foster their own curiosity and willingness to move toward belongingness.

3. **Function** . . . (e.g., point toward a function) that is currently lacking (or more that is needed) within the belongingness activity, event, group, or relationship. Suggest that the belongingness "thing" is in need. Say that it's "interesting" or "a coincidence" that the very thing that is lacking is the sort of thing the client possesses/is aligned with. Pause here and let things lie. Do NOT tell the client they "should" belong and insert themselves. Let them give at least some faint indication that they want to.

4. **Explore** . . . and learn more about the belongingness possibility. Do not pounce on this spark of curiosity and engagement. Gently offer your willingness to help them learn more about it. Offer to research/look into it more WITH the client. Ask them for ideas about how you both might learn more about it (e.g., "Do you think there might be any

websites we could find/YouTube® videos with kids who are already doing it, and we could find out what they think of it?").

5. **Reveal** ... (once the client is showing some momentum of engagement/willingness to explore) with authentic self-disclosure how you—being someone "who's gotten to know them a bit"—believe they would really like the item, and that you think it's awesome that he/she is up for checking this out more. Make this step fit the child in terms of how "thick" you lay out the self-disclosure. You don't want to snuff out the embers of engagement with too much long-winded blowing.

Leap (Into Action)

Again, you are not hammering them toward doing things or trying to make it happen. Instead, you are very mindful of your own experience AND theirs; you're inviting them toward possibilities and providing them structure and assistance in moving forward into what is truly anxiety-provoking and soaked in a feeling of risk.

Resurrect the visualization of your sample client (or conjure another child in need of belongingness). How might you make them an OFFER of belonging? Plan your intervention:

O _____

F _____

F _____

E _____

R _____

Channeling Your "Inner Supervisor"

Get Oriented

Particularly in working with kids who push, pull, blame, and shut down, it can easily feel daunting, if not downright desperate, to get the client's work moving in a positive, productive direction. Clinicians burn out and lose the light that likely directed them to their clinical path in the first place with enough episodes of feeling lost, ineffective, and overwhelmed. In short, it's easy to lose your sense of meaningful purpose in working with challenging kids whose behavior is reflective of how little of it they have themselves. This brief practice is meant to remind you to pick yourself up and move toward what matters. It does so by reminding you of someone who has done that for you in the past.

Listen (To What Actually IS)

1. Bring to mind some of your recent work with an EBD child client that didn't go as well as you'd planned. Perhaps it felt "disastrous" to you.

2. Notice any resistance, both physical and emotional, to calling this client and the situation back up in memory.

3. Allow yourself to conjure as many specific details about this situation and client as you can, checking in with multiple senses, and notice what emerges. Breathe slowly and allow the scene to deepen in your awareness.

Look (To the Fit of Intervention with the Moment)

- If you were channeling your favorite training-days supervisor, what might you say to a supervisee who was doing what you did and facing what you faced in that situation? With what sort of tone would you say it to them? How would you regard any judgment or self-criticism the supervisee was directing toward themselves?

Leap (Into Action)

■ Try directing your former supervisor's sentiments toward yourself *now*. Say these words to yourself, perhaps even out loud! Notice how this feels and continue to watch any resistance.

■ Take an action that dovetails with these words as soon as possible (a.k.a. now). Perhaps even write a "session note" about this client interaction and do so from the perspective of your inner supervisor. How might your work with this client shift going forward?

Finally, try the following steps to help make the PURE skills a more fluid, daily part of your therapy. This sequence outlines the core process for integrating these psychological, emotional, and behavioral skills into who you are:

1. **Seeing the change:** Identify a model. Who is someone you admire who has demonstrated proficiency with the PURE skill you're working on? Make this person your internal surrogate. Visualize how this person would handle specific situations using the skill you're looking to develop. Imagine the person performing this action in vivid, sensory detail. Next, try on similar behaviors: visualize replacing this surrogate with yourself and watch the mental movie of yourself mastering this skill.

2. **Doing the change:** Even if your performance falls short of your visualization, put the PURE skill into action at the next available opportunity. Don't be down on yourself for any perceived failure. Use mindfulness to wade through such reactions.

3. **Reviewing the change:** Track your progress in a journal. Get regular feedback on your development of the skill from those you trust to be brutally yet compassionately honest with you.

4. **Being the change:** Integrate this skill into a new definition of your therapy. Don't view this skill as merely a behavior pattern you adopted. View it as part of who you are as a clinician and a person more generally. Celebrate your progress. Give yourself the credit you deserve for this work on behalf of your clients.

Finding Your True North as a Clinician

Get Oriented

A Chinese proverb tells us "pearls don't lie on the seashore. If you want one, you must dive for it." Working from our values entails taking a risk. We risk the pain of falling short in our clinical work. These are not goals, not things you check off your to-do list so you can move on. They're things you can keep showing up to do and that you do simply because they matter. These are true directions, like headings on a compass. You're never really done with these; rather, you just keep moving in these directions. Instead of outcomes like consistent school attendance or using problem-solving skills at home (great as goals for your work with child clients, but NOT behaviors of *yours* you can show up to that make your daily work meaningful) seek patterns of behavior like creativity, consistent attunement to client's discomfort, and mentoring. No one needs to convince you of your list of professional values because they just matter. You're never "done" with them. There's no to-do list you check off and no performance evaluation or managed care form that holds you accountable for them. When it comes to the values driving your daily work, ultimately, you're only accountable to yourself.

Listen (To What Actually IS)

Try this brief visualization exercise: Imagine you're sitting in a large ballroom. You can hear the pleasant commotion of dinner conversations and convivial laughter. You're about to go to the dessert table for a slice of something egregious when someone starts clinking a glass. You look around and notice that everyone is looking at you. Thankfully, you notice they're all smiling, and yet you feel the pressure of the moment. Don't worry, though—you won't have to give a speech. Not yet. Instead, people you know very well are coming up to the podium on the stage and looking at you as they approach the microphone.

"Let me tell you a bit about our friend here," they say, pointing at you. "Let me tell you about the sort of professional I had the privilege of working with all these years."

It's your retirement gathering, and the people coming one at a time to the podium are the colleagues (and maybe a few clients) who feel compelled to speak about the impact of your work. They are looking right at you and telling this room full of friends, family, and colleagues what things you showed up to across the many years of your work that resonated with them. They're giving examples of the sorts of actions you took—the things you were willing to do—that simply mattered.

Let yourself really conjure the scene in your mind's eye. Let your mind loosen and allow the situation to play out like a movie in your imagination.

And now ask yourself: What would you ideally like to hear these people say about you? What patterns of action would you have them notice? What VALUES (patterns of behavior) were you willing to show up to over and over that may not have made you perfect, but made your work personally meaningful?

There's no right answer here. Your professional values are yours and yours alone. Your work, particularly challenging work such as that we're addressing in this book, can flourish if you make the effort to flesh out and consistently enact the values that drew you into this field in the first place.

Look (To the Fit of Intervention with the Moment)

Becoming clear on what matters most for you will not only deepen your work satisfaction, but it will also help prevent burnout and make your interventions much more effective. The core values behind your decisions as a clinician—including your missteps—can help pull you forward and help you answer yes to the "am I willing?" question when faced with challenges in working with EBD clients. After you've worked to identify these values and make them accessible, in challenging moments they can become a sort of magnetic north, offering you guidance.

To help you identify the values that give your professional work direction, let's take a quick detour from your work-a-day world and go back to school.

Your Greatest Teacher

1. Sit in a quiet place and close your eyes. Take a breath and remember how your breathing has always been there inside and around you. Your breath is your constant companion, there to help your body adjust to whatever the situation requires.

2. When you were a kid in school, there was a teacher who really mattered to you. The teacher you most admired. The teacher who had the greatest positive impact on you. Let your mind gravitate toward this teacher. Imagine this person clearly, using multiple senses. Remember exactly what the teacher did or said that hit the mark for you.

3. What, specifically, were their actions toward you? What qualities kept showing up in the teacher's teaching and interactions? Don't just think about it; allow yourself to really feel answers as they show up.

4. Open your eyes. Note these specific actions and qualities in a journal. Write down as many things that made this teacher special for you as possible.

5. Pause for a moment and notice how you feel. What's showing up for you as you remember this teacher? To what degree did you want to perform well for this person? To what degree did you want to be in this person's presence? How much did you end up learning?

6. Notice the qualities you listed in step 4. How important are these for *you* to embody in your role as a professional NOW? If they're important to you *and* you embody them, what might be the impact on your clients?

7. Consider embracing your teacher's qualities as guiding values for you as a professional.

We're working here to identify and create more ready avenues for you to access these values. No one and no book can create these values for you—they are already there. If you are willing to understand what they have to show you, these values are ready to guide you. Authenticity, compassion, perseverance, generosity—whatever they are, you need only be willing to let yourself move toward them when opportunities arise.

Leap (Into Action)

Now try the following exercise to help galvanize your guiding values into daily action:

Look at the fingers of one of your hands. The thumb is your "intention"—your desire to open yourself to the core values that guide your work. Your thumb can reach out and touch the tips of each of the other fingers on the hand—these other four fingers are the "reasons," the shared values, for where the work is going that are coiled up and temporarily lost when pulled into a fist.

In a mere moment, your intending thumb can silently reach out and lightly touch each of these reasons, these values for pursuing the work with challenging child or teen clients and their families. With four quick taps, your hand can release the memory of what you gain by letting go in the direction of these values.

List four valued directions for your work (either specific to the work with clients or in general regarding your role as a clinician). In what direction might your work go despite all the difficulty along long the way? Focus less on specific outcomes and more on ongoing processes or qualities that the work can cultivate. List your best "four fingers"—reasons for opening within the work—in the following spaces:

1. _____

2. _____

3. _____

4. _____

During a time of reflection or mindful checking regarding your caseload, take a few minutes and assign each reason to a finger and, touching it with your thumb, hold it in the center of your awareness. Let any thoughts, sensations, images, or emotions arise and fall away. Stay focused on this reason, coming back to it as many times as necessary to enliven and elaborate it. Focus your attention on each reason until your awareness rests fully and completely within it for a time, and then move to the next finger.

Once you have established a clear connection to your reasons, your values, for doing your work, you will be ready to bring these reasons to bear during actual interactions. In fact, nothing is more real than your reasons—it is the chaotic ebb and flow of daily life that is less real.

When in the course of work with challenging child clients or during a time when you're finding yourself gripping thoughts and reactions in your work, mindfully remember your four fingers. If you are willing, bring the intention of your thumb silently and gently to each of your four fingertips in slow succession. See what happens if you choose to fully connect, in the moment of reflexive tightening, with your reasons for what matters most in your work. Each time you meet a particularly vexing client, or anytime you find yourself heading into a clinical interaction with less than ample enthusiasm, begin the interaction with a quick thumb-to-finger tap. Notice how quickly you can call up and access the values always lying underneath the surface. If you really give this practice a serious try, my bet is you'll never tap thumb to finger again without these values leaping forward for you.

Are you willing to let your values guide your next day's work? Take a moment and end with a quick breathing practice to galvanize the benefits of bringing attention to your core professional values:

1. Sitting upright with your eyes closed, call to mind a recent interaction with an EBD child client that went extremely well, where you connected or shared in something meaningful or fun. Even if the work didn't go as well as planned, perhaps focus in on work with a client in which, regardless of the outcome, it simply mattered (to you, and perhaps to the child as well).

2. As the image of this situation appears, notice the sensations in your body.

3. For 10 breaths, sit with that image and any sensations or thoughts that arise.

4. Count each breath gently and silently, keeping your focus on the experience of that experience.

5. Open your eyes and notice how you feel. Truly savor this experience for its meaning and resonance.

Repeat these steps. This time, call to mind a recent exchange with either this or another client that did *not* go well, one that may have involved considerable intensity and pain for both of you. Notice what arises. Stay with this as you count out 10 breaths. Don't worry about breathing in any particular way; simply notice the breath moving in and out as you focus on the images and sensations from the situation.

Ask yourself: At the close of just these 10 breaths, have the images and sensations of this tough episode remained exactly the same in quality and content? Have they changed on their own?

Fueling Purpose

My "What Matters" in This Moment Compass

Chapter 10

Focusing on Process vs. Outcome in Work

with EDB Child and Teen Clients

PRINCIPLE 10.1

Hold All Desired Outcomes Lightly

What (It Is)

We signed up to be "change agents" because we want to help people change for the better—we want to create positive outcomes for them. Here's the thing: How much do you actually have control over *any* outcome for your clients? What happens the more you try to exert control over what happens in their lives? What if you more consistently let go of *believing* you can call the shots for clients and instead show up with great effort and yet flexibility that allows you to do so without fixating on making things change? Here, we take a brief, yet crucial look at the power of having goals but not shoving them into the air between you and your young clients.

Why (It Matters)

As a Boy Scout, I was taught to make sure you clear the area you intend to use for your campfire of any brush, leaves, or anything combustible. Only when things are cleared should you set about building your fire (that is, if you want to have any control over preventing a forest fire!). And yet, no matter how much you clear the area, no matter how combustible the kindling, and no matter how many times you've made campfires in the past, can you control the exact timing and nature of any resulting flame? (The answer is no!) It is the same for building the ideal conditions for change to spark for your EBD child clients—particularly those "empathy hard" among them—the ones who act out, push back, and lash out the most. You have to clear away the brush, the clutter of your expectations in order to best create the conditions of positive change.

When or Where (It Applies)

It is crucial for you to learn to work from an "agenda-less" orientation, especially with the most challenging clients. It's not that your goals are irrelevant. You just have to hold them *lightly*—on the palm of your hand, not gripped in a change-greedy fist. If you're not gripping anything, it's much harder for clients to play tug-of-war with you. In doing this agenda-less accepting, you are strengthening your perspective muscle. You can't see the client clearly (and they won't feel like they've been truly noticed) if you're always looking over their shoulder and down the road.

How (To Cultivate It)

Think of a sample EBD client—the more challenging their presentation, the better. Queue this child up vividly in your mind's eye. With the client firmly in mind, ask yourself: What is it specifically, in your best professional opinion as a helper, that your client needs to do (or not do) in order to make progress, to move their lives forward? List your top five "EBD client to-do or not-do" conclusion:

1. _____

2. _____

3. _____

4. _____

5. _____

Review your list. These things make complete sense, don't they? You are highly trained and have significant experience working with these sorts of issues, right? *Of course,* this plan is reasonable. You know this client and their clinical context well, and you're certain that if they could start doing or not doing these things, things would improve.

Now try this: Take a pen, the darker and thicker the ink, the better. Don't use a pencil—this needs to be permanent. Look at your top-five list and one by one, cross out each item. Pause and consider each one as you cross it out. These things are GONE. I've consulted my "crystal ball" and I've seen the future down the tracks of your work with this client; these things are NOT ever going to happen. Close your eyes, and use mindfulness to observe your experience of the "reality" that these things will never happen. What shows up in your thoughts and feelings? Do you notice any tugging toward reactivity? How much do you want to control what happens for your client? Just allow yourself to notice this pull of understanding desire, and watch what it does *inside* you.

If you invested in your work with this particular client, an exercise such as the one you just completed creates a fair amount of dissonance—put more bluntly, it doesn't feel so good. It hurts a bit to let go of "necessary" outcomes for clients. These things make complete sense based on your years of training and experience. Of course, clients should march enthusiastically in the direction of these changes, but you cannot control whether this happens. It's just your dissonance—more specifically, your drive to avoid feeling "not good" about things not turning out well for clients—that gets in the way of your best, most effective work.

Putting Discomfort on Ice

Get Oriented

Among school, sports, peers, family, and oh, yes—therapy—EBD child and teen clients these days have many reasons for getting stressed. This activity serves as both a way to engage ("touch to engage") clients and will also serve as a metaphor in your work with them regarding the power of hanging in with physical and emotional discomfort despite what their reactive thoughts might say. It will help you give them some practice melting away stress and riding out emotional intensity in a fun, challenging way.

Listen (To What Actually IS)

- Set a timer for between three and five minutes.

- Get an ice cube (a small one, and one for everyone participating, including you) and sit in a quiet place. Hold the cube in an open hand and simply look at it. Have kids hold their hands out in the air between you, so that you're leaning toward each other, looking at your respective ice cubes together. Hang in there and breathe deeply and slowly, letting the air fill your belly.

- Notice all the sensations in your hand—stinging, burning, pulsing—whatever is here; just feel it WITHOUT moving or doing anything if you can. Encourage kids to speak out loud as to the sensations and the thoughts that show up while they're holding the ice cube.

Look (To the Fit of Intervention with the Moment)

- Hold your ice cubes without dropping them or setting them down while the timer is counting down. What do people notice? What's happening to the ice when you don't even do anything? Are things changing? Do you have to do anything for the ice to melt (change) on its own? Encourage kids to keep up the deep, slow breathing.

- *Ask kids:* "Does your brain tell you to drop it or throw it away? See if you're willing to keep on holding it anyway."

- Have kids notice how discomfort doesn't have to be something to struggle against. We can learn to watch it with mindfulness and do things that are important anyway.

Leap (Into Action)

In this activity, your client(s) (and you!) have to deal with something hard (like cold ice on your hand). Sometimes stress or emotions are like that. We get upset, our bodies get tense, and we walk around feeling frozen. We may even try to force ourselves to feel better by playing really hard, blaming or poking at others, or "freezing up" in front of the TV.

Here, you've helped kids learn that if they pause and focus on the sensations in their bodies and the thoughts passing by, "stressful feelings" and intense emotions can and WILL (just like the cold of ice) change on their own.

Yes, it's important for your clients to learn problem-solving skills and ways to take action to address challenges and manage stressors, but sometimes (particularly once uncomfortable feelings are already here) it can help to simply stop, quit forcing things, and remind them that by simply paying attention and noticing, painful experiences actually shift inside us on their own. Yes, teach kids to do things to change their situations for the better, but it's crucial to teach them how to ride out emotional discomfort without flinching or flailing out at others.

When the chips are down and there's no immediate solution to a situation, are your clients able to learn to put emotional pain "on ice" and allow the pain to change on its own?

Learning to do so helps clear their mindsets so that when a possible solution to difficulty arrives on the scene, they are sufficiently aware and emotionally available to see it and take a leap in its direction.

Jumping Jack the Pirate and Dropping an Anchor in a Storm

Get Oriented

Find me someone who has never become emotionally overwhelmed—tossed about emotionally in some tough situation—and I'll offer up proof to the world of the existence of zombies. You'd literally need to be "undead" to not experience emotions at this intensity, at least occasionally. This is actually a self-evident point that is helpful to review with your EBD child clients who, at times, believe they are the only humans in history to get so swept up in their feelings and tossed about with "bad" behavior. Help them learn to drop an anchor amid their emotional storms, and you'll do them a significant therapeutic service. Here's how to do it (and teach it)

Listen (To What Actually IS)

Show Up

1. Set a timer for no more than one or two minutes and focus attention on the sensations of breathing, wherever you feel them most notably.

2. Reset the timer for another minute and notice sensations in your body; whatever pops up most prominently is fine. And then do the same with the sounds occurring around you, wherever you are.

3. Now—*as weird as it sounds*—stand up and do at least 30 jumping jacks!! If you're in a group, set a timer and see who can do the most in one full minute. Ready, set, jack it up!!

Look (To the Fit of Intervention with the Moment)
Shut Up (and Pay Attention)

1. If the giggles have set in, that's fine—just allow yourself to settle into quiet. If you're breathing hard, that's fine, too! You're in a physical "storm" of sorts, and you're a bit worked up. Immediately sit back down, close your eyes, and bring your spine upright and alert.

2. If sitting in a chair, press your feet into the floor beneath you. If you're sitting on the floor, try pressing your hands into the floor instead. You're dropping an "anchor." Keep pressing and anchor your attention to the sensations of your hands or feet pressing into the ground.

3. Pay attention to your mind wandering to your still-fast-beating heart, a bead of sweat, that stirred-up-stormy-feeling inside. If you're distracted away for a moment, no worries; just bring your focus back to your anchor—the feeling of pressing into the ground. You can't control what's happening around you, and you can't flick a switch and simply turn off how your body is feeling, BUT you can keep connected to your anchor. Just like for a boat in a storm, an anchor can keep you from getting completely blown away until the storm passes on its own.

Leap (Into Action)
Put Up

1. Open your eyes, take a full, deep breath, and stand up.

2. Immediately let yourself start doing something that requires focus—even if it is tying your shoes! The point here is to experience what it's like to have dropped an anchor when you were stirred up and to have chosen to have done so from a place of mindfulness.

3. Do things turn out better or worse when you drop an anchor before trying to deal with a stormy situation and its stirred up feelings in your body and thoughts in your mind? What's it like to realize you may not be able to control the storms, but you can control how you ride them out? What might happen if you were willing to consistently implement this new habit?

Sidestepping Stories

Get Oriented

No clinician is immune—particularly those brave souls hardy enough to work with EBD children and teens. We all end up getting bound up and limited by our internal narratives, about who we are as helpers and as people more generally. Humans are verbal, meaning-making creatures, and as so, our brains are always using words and images to derive a sensible tale as to why things are happening, what the causes are, and what might be done about it. Our ability to do so has allowed us as a species to dominate this planet (for good or for ill, depending on your perspective!). We are not the biggest and strongest animal out there, but our ability to harness language to symbolize our experience—to think beyond the actual sensory realities of the present moment—has allowed us to paint the ceiling of the Sistine Chapel, write "Hamlet," cure polio, and summit Everest. But here's the downside: Our wordiness is the source of most (arguably ALL) of our suffering.

Why? Because we buy into our verbal stories as true, sometimes even if they run counter to the facts of the world around us or our own bodily experience. Though our internal story-making is a crucial part of who we are, we should see it for what it really is: brain-based guessing with words and mental pictures. Our stories should ideally be viewed as tools to help us achieve goals and manage challenges. They should not be verbal handcuffs binding up our ability to be effective, compassionate, and feel satisfied and competent in our work.

Listen (To What Actually IS)

It's very likely that in the course of your clinical work you've heard a client say the following:

"I am depressed."

Though it's certainly important for clients to acknowledge and face their challenges, does it open up or constrict their lives if they move through their day buying into that statement? Inside them (and perhaps out loud as well) it will sound like this:

"I AM depressed."

The point here is that if we operate from the frame that our inner language IS reality, it cuts us off from possibilities and from seeing clearly what else is happening. Depressive thinking breeds depressive action and more of the same. The same is true with anxiety. The same is true with your language about *yourself* as a clinician. When you are working with challenging clients, all manner of self-judgment, doubt, and negativity somehow go from mental fiction to gospel truth in your mind. Let's listen for just this sort of story-making.

Consider a negative view you have of some aspect of your work or performance.

- Are you willing to merely notice that this is a negatively-toned story you are thinking now in this moment?

- Write the thought on a sheet of paper and sit looking at the words. Breathe slowly and deeply and recognize the fact that these words are just that—words—and that you are also breathing, sitting, hearing, and basically experiencing all sorts of things in this moment with as much (if not more) validity as those words.

- Are you willing to *have* this story instead of *being* it?

Look (To the Fit of Intervention with the Moment)

- Which way of relating to the story opens things up for you in your work with specific clients? What does your experience say rather than your mind/more thoughts?

- What other negative stories might you be holding onto?

Leap (Into Action)

We go to the theater to see scripted interactions between characters. We can do better in our real, professional (and personal) lives. We can improvise if we choose. Ask yourself: Am I willing to create a new relationship with my experience of my most challenging EBD child client *right now*? Your answer will determine whether perhaps old, less-than-ideally effective patterns continue in your work or you take a new step forward. We can write new scripts for how we want to handle the emotions cropping up in our most challenging work. As we do, others—especially our clients—will notice us doing so. Even our small actions can have significant positive ripple effects.

Consider journaling for a few minutes. What old pattern—perhaps a negative cycle—has recently surfaced in your interactions with a particular client? As you write, note the thoughts, feelings, and even actions that arise. Is it easy or difficult to stay with whatever your mind shares? If it's difficult, are you willing to stay with it anyway?

Consider again for a moment: What happens to your part of the pattern when you rest in the skills of mindfulness discussed throughout this book? What will happen if you intervene with your clients from a foundation of these?

- What might you do right now that runs counter to the words in this story about yourself and the client? For example, if you're thinking says that you can't help a particular client, how might you do something NOW that serves this person? If your story says that you're really not that good at limit-setting, what action can you take to improve your skills regardless of these thoughts? You get the point: Make it a habit to take your self-judgmental and self-limiting thoughts "under advisement," but don't regard them as stone-carved commandments.

Take Self-Compassion to Heart

Get Oriented

It's not just our clients who ruminate negatively about themselves—it could be me, for instance, telling myself over and over that I'm an "absolute failure" as a therapist for not paying attention to a client for a split second during a session or eviscerating a future version of myself based on a minor faux pas last week. Rumination is the run-on self-talk of the mind that has agitated energy as both its fuel and its output. Ruminative thinking is toxic to our well-being and clarity of mind.

So how do we work with rumination? One way forward is self-compassion. Self-compassion is far more than chasing rainbows and skipping after unicorns. According to psychologist and researcher Kristin Neff, self-compassion is self-kindness (versus self-judgment) combined with a sense of common humanity (versus being alone with what's hard) and mindfulness (versus being over-identified with bad feelings).[25] Self-compassion is seeing our pain as part of the larger, universal picture of being human and seeing ourselves as worthy of kindness and care. It's not weak or passive or narcissistic and self-indulgent. It takes guts to practice, and science shows that it can do much to lower anxiety, stress reactions, depression, and perfectionism. It can open you up to your life whereas your old patterns or reaction and self-judgment close you down.

Listen (To What Actually IS)

- Bring to mind a recent mistake or misstep you made in the course of your work.

- Notice how you feel in your body as you recall the moment. Focus in and let yourself mentally inventory the sensations showing up as you remember (in detail) what happened.

Look (To the Fit of Intervention with the Moment)

- Place a hand on your heart and try out saying the following:

- "Making mistakes is stressful and causes me discomfort."

- "All clinicians at all stages of their work make mistakes and feel discomfort as a result."

- "May I learn from this and move on, and I hope all those who work with EBD clients do the same."

Leap (Into Action)

- Do something today that focuses on taking care of YOU.

- Shift from any experience of shame for your mistake toward a healthy sense of actionable regret. By this, I mean note to yourself that your mistake was an "unskillful" action, and imagine yourself exhibiting a more skillful response in a similar situation in the future.

- Acknowledge your error to a trusted colleague and let them know what you've learned for future situations. Rest assured that not only are you benefiting yourself, but by talking openly and self-compassionately about a past error, you are helping your colleague as well. You are modeling the power of authenticity and a willingness to face the obvious fact of professional imperfection.

Appendix

Books and Articles

Abblett, M. A. (2017). *Helping your angry teen: How to reduce anger and build connection using mindfulness and positive psychology*. Oakland: New Harbinger.

Abblett, M. A. (2016). *Mindfulness for teen depression: A workbook for improving your mood*. Oakland: New Harbinger.

Abblett, M. A. (2013). *The heat of the moment in treatment: Mindful management of difficult clients*. New York: Norton.

Aggs, C., & Bambling, M. (2010). Teaching mindfulness to psychotherapists in clinical practice: The mindful therapy programme. *Counselling and Psychotherapy Research, 10*, 278–286.

Arch, J., Eifert, G. H., Davies, C., Vilardaga, J. P., Rose, R. D., & Craske, M. G. (2012). Randomized clinical trial of cognitive behavioral therapy (CBT) versus acceptance and commitment therapy (ACT) for mixed anxiety disorders. *Journal of Consulting and Clinical Psychology, 80*(5), 750–765.

Baer, R. A. (2003). Mindfulness training as a clinical intervention: A conceptual and empirical review. *Clinical Psychology: Science and Practice, 10*, 125–143.

Berne, E. (1964). *Games people play*. New York: Grove.

Bohlmeijer, E. T., Fledderus, M., Rokx, T. A. & Pieterse, M. E. (2011). Efficacy of an early intervention based on acceptance and commitment therapy for adults with depressive symptomatology: Evaluation in a randomized controlled trial. *Behavior Research and Therapy, 49*, 62–67.

Bowen, S., Witkiewitz, K., Dillworth, T. M., & Marlatt, G. A. (2007). The role of thought suppression in the relationship between mindfulness meditation and alcohol use. *Addictive Behaviors, 32*, 2324–2328.

Brassell, A. A., Rosenberg, E., Parent, J., Rough, J. N., Fondacaro, K., & Seehuus, M. (2016). Parent's psychological flexibility: Associations with parenting and child psychosocial well-being. *Journal of Contextual Behavioral Science, 5*, 111–120.

Bruce, N. G., Manber, R., Shapiro, S. L., & Constantino, M. J. (2010). Psychotherapist mindfulness and the psychotherapy process. *Psychotherapy: Theory, Research, Practice and Training, 47*, 83–97.

Cappas, N. M., Andres-Hyman, R., & Davidson, L. (2005). What psychotherapists can begin to learn from neuroscience: Seven principles of brain-based psychotherapy. *Psychotherapy, 42*, 374–383.

Christopher, J. C., & Maris, J. A. (2010). Integrating mindfulness as self-care into counseling and psychotherapy training. *Counselling and Psychotherapy Research, 10*(2), 114–125.

Croskerry, P. (2003). The importance of cognitive errors in diagnosis and strategies to minimize them. *Academic Medicine, 78,* 775–780.

Clarke, S., Taylor, G., Lancaster, J., & Remington, B. (2015). Acceptance and commitment therapy-based self-management versus psychoeducation training for staff caring for clients with a personality disorder: A randomized controlled trial. *Journal of Personality Disorders, 29,* 163–176.

Dixon, M. R., Wilson, A. N., & Habib, R. (2016). Neurological evidence of acceptance and commitment therapy effectiveness in college-age gamblers. *Journal of Contextual Behavioral Science, 5,* 80–88.

Dobson, K. S., Hollon, S. D., Dimidjian, S., Schmaling, K. B., Kohlenberg, R. J., Gallop, R. J., et al. (2008). Randomized trial of behavioral activation, cognitive therapy, and antidepressant medication in the prevention of relapse and recurrence in major depression. *Journal of Consulting and Clinical Psychology, 76*(3), 468–477.

Flückiger, C., Del Re, A. C., Wampold, B. E., Symonds, D., & Horvath, A. O. (2011). How central is the alliance in psychotherapy? A multilevel longitudinal meta-analysis. *Journal of Counseling Psychology, 59*(1), 10–17.

Forman, E. M., Hoffman, K. L., Juarascio, A. S., Butryn, M. L., & Herbert, J. D. (2013). Comparison of acceptance-based and standard cognitive-based coping strategies for craving sweets in overweight and obese women. *Eating Behaviors, 14,* 64–68.

Foreman, S. A., & Marmar, C. R. (1985). Therapist actions that address initially poor therapeutic alliances in psychotherapy. *American Journal of Psychiatry, 142,* 922–926.

Gelso, C., & Hayes, J. (2007). *Countertransference and the therapist's inner experience: Perils and possibilities.* Mahwah, NJ: Erlbaum.

Goldstein, J. (1993). *Insight meditation: The practice of freedom.* Boston: Shambhala.

Gottman, J. M. (1999). *The marriage clinic: A scientifically based marital therapy.* New York: Norton.

Gloster, A. T., Sonntag, R., Hoyer, J., Meyer, A. H., Heinze, S., Ströhle, A., & Wittchen, H. U. (2015). Treating treatment-resistant patients with panic disorder and agoraphobia using psychotherapy: A randomized controlled switching trial. *Psychotherapy and Psychosomatics, 84*(2), 100–109.

Hann, K. E. J., & McCracken, L. M. (2014). A systematic review of randomized controlled trials of acceptance and commitment therapy for adults with chronic pain: Outcome domains, design quality, and efficacy. *Journal of Contextual Behavioral Science, 3,* 217–227.

Harris, R. (2009). *ACT made simple: A quick-start guide to ACT basics and beyond.* Oakland, CA: New Harbinger.

Hayes, S. C., & Smith, S. (2005). *Get out of your mind and into your life: The new acceptance and commitment therapy.* Oakland, CA: New Harbinger.

Hayes, S. C., Stroshahl, K., & Wilson, K. G. (1999). *Acceptance and commitment therapy: An experiential approach to behavior change.* New York: Guilford.

Kopp, S. (1977). *Back to one: A practical guide for psychotherapists.* Palo Alto, CA: Science and Behavior Books.

Minahan, J., & Rappaport, N. (2012). *The behavior code: A practical guide to understanding and teaching the most challenging students.* Cambridge, MA: Harvard Education Press.

Muran, J. C., & Barber, J. P. (Eds.) (2010). *The therapeutic alliance: An evidence-based guide to practice.* New York: Guilford.

Roffey, S. (2013). Inclusive and exclusive belonging: The impact on individual and community well-being. *Educational and Child Psychology, 30*(1), 38–49.

Safran, J., & Muran, C. (2000). *Negotiating the therapeutic alliance: A relational treatment guide.* New York: Guilford.

Schneider, W. J., Cavell, T., & Hughes, J. (2003). A sense of containment: Potential moderator of the relation between parenting practices and children's externalizing behaviors. *Development and Psychopathology, 15,* 95–117.

Seigel, D. J. (2010). *The mindful therapist: A clinician's guide to mindsight and neural integration.* New York: Norton.

Wachtel, P. (2008). *Relational theory and the practice of psychotherapy.* New York: Guilford.

Wicks, R. (2008). *The resilient clinician.* New York: Oxford University Press.

Willard, C. W. (2017*). Raising resilience: The wisdom and science of happy families and thriving children.* Boulder, CO: Sounds True.

Willard, C. W. & Saltzman, A. (Eds.) (2015). *Teaching mindfulness skills to kids and teens.* New York: Guilford.

Wilson, K. G. (2008). *Mindfulness for two: An acceptance and commitment therapy approach to mindfulness in psychotherapy.* Oakland, CA: New Harbinger.

Mobile Apps

Headspace
www.getsomeheadspace.com
Insight Timer (meditation timer)
https://insighttimer.com
Stop, Breathe and Think
www.app.stopbreaththink.org

Card Decks of Coping Skills Practices

Growing Mindful: Mindfulness Practices for All Ages. PESI Publishing and Media.
http://amzn.to/2G3ajg3
Growing Happy: Positive Psychology Practices for Teens and Adults. PESI Publishing and Media.
http://amzn.to/2BmCqYw

Websites

https://ibme.info/about/

Inward Bound Mindfulness Education (iBme) is a nonprofit that offers in-depth mindfulness programming for youth and the parents and professionals who support them. Our programming guides teens and young adults in developing self-awareness, compassion, and ethical decision making, and empowers them to apply these skills in improving their lives and communities.

https://www.naset.org/emotionaldisturbance2.0.html

The National Association of Special Education Teachers (NASET) is a national membership organization dedicated to rendering all possible support and assistance to those preparing for or teaching in the field of special education. NASET was founded to promote the profession of special education teachers and to provide a national forum for their ideas.

www.mindfuled.org

Mindfulness in Education Network (MiEN) was established in 2001 by a group of educators, students of Thich Nhat Hanh, Zen Master and peace activist. Hanh was nominated for the Nobel Peace Prize by Dr. Martin Luther King, Jr. We see mindfulness as an antidote to the growing stress, conflict, and confusion in educational settings, as well as an invaluable gift to give students. Our network currently consists of more than 1,700 members nationally and internationally.

https://childmind.org/about-us/

The Child Mind Institute is an independent, national nonprofit dedicated to transforming the lives of children and families struggling with mental health and learning disorders. Our teams work every day to deliver the highest standards of care, advance the science of the developing brain, and empower parents, professionals, and policymakers to support children when and where they need it most.

http://www.ccbd.net/about/aboutus

Council for Children with Behavioral Disorders (CCBD) is an international community of educators that is the voice and vision of special education for children and youth with or at risk of emotional and behavioral disorders. CCBD is a diverse, vibrant professional organization that works together and with others to ensure that these students are valued and included in all aspects of life.

https://jbcc.harvard.edu/about

Judge Baker Children's Center (Judge Baker) is a nonprofit organization that serves children by promoting their developmental, emotional, and intellectual well-being. With a century of proven leadership in children's mental health issues, Judge Baker helps children and families chart their own best course to grow and thrive.

https://centerforadolescentstudies.com

The Center for Adolescent Studies is an interdisciplinary training institute providing high-quality training for professionals working with adolescents. Our mission is to train adults to help teens thrive through in-person and online professional development and continuing education training.

http://www.childtrauma.org/

Child Trauma Academy. Led by renowned researcher Bruce Perry, the Child Trauma Academy seeks to improve the lives of high-risk children through direct service, research, and education by creating biologically-informed child and family respectful practice, programs, and policy.

http://learn.nctsn.org/course/category.php?id=3

Learning Center for Child and Adolescent Trauma provides free access to NCTSN experts and up-to-date, science-based information in the areas of assessment, treatment and services, training, research and evaluation, and organizational and systems change for traumatized children, adolescents, and their families.

http://www.starrtraining.org/tlc

The mission of the **National Institute for Trauma and Loss in Children (TLC)** is to bring out the best in every traumatized child by creating environments where children can flourish. This site contains information about traumatized children and adults, as well as resources and training.

http://www.ptsd.va.gov/

National Post Traumatic Stress Network. This website has numerous fact sheets, assessment instruments, and articles on trauma in areas of children, adolescents, adults, family, active military, and veterans. It includes free online instruction to help provide a basic understanding of Post-Traumatic Stress Disorder (PTSD).

http://www.sanctuaryweb.com/Documents/Sanctuary%20in%20the%20School.pdf

Creating Sanctuary in Schools describes the basis for the process of providing a safe and healing environment for children in schools who need to recover from the effects of trauma, as well as for less traumatized children. Basic assumptions, values, goals, and the process that must be shared by all members of the system are described.

http://www.massadvocates.org/download-book.php

Helping Traumatized Children Learn demonstrates how children's trauma from exposure to family and other forms of violence can help explain many educational difficulties teachers face every day. Such difficulties include the inability of children to focus, understand instructions, form meaningful relationships with peers and teachers, and control their behavior in appropriate ways. The report provides a school-wide flexible framework and a public policy agenda for creating trauma-sensitive school environments where traumatized children and their classmates can focus, behave, and learn.

http://k12.wa.us/CompassionateSchools/HeartofLearning.aspx

The Heart of Learning: Compassion, Resiliency, and Academic Success is a handbook written and compiled by the State of Washington Office of the Superintendent of Public Instruction and Western Washington University staff. It contains valuable information for educators to help them on a daily basis as they work with students whose learning has been adversely impacted by trauma in their lives.

Notes

1. Gilbert, D. T., & Malone, P. S. (1995). The correspondence bias. *Psychological Bulletin, 117,* 21–38.
2. Gottman, J. M. (2002). *The relationship cure.* New York: Three Rivers Press.
3. Croskerry, P. (2003). The importance of cognitive errors in diagnosis and strategies to minimize them. *Journal of Academic Medicine, 78,* 775–780.
4. Van Dillen, L. F., Heslenfeld, D. J., & Koole, S. L. (2009). Tuning down the emotional brain: An fMRI study of the effects of cognitive load on the processing of affective images. *Neuroimage, 45,* 1212–1219.
5. Patterson, G. R. (1982). *Coercive family process.* Eugene, OR: Castalia.
6. Granic, I., & Patterson, G. R. (2006). Toward a comprehensive model of antisocial development: A dynamic systems approach. *Psychological Review, 113*(1), 101–131.
7. Tronick, E., Als, H., Adamson, L., Wise, S., & Brazelton, B. (1978). The infant's response to entrapment between contradictory messages in face-to-face interaction. *American Academy of Child Psychiatry, 1,* 1–13.
8. Gorman-Barry, P. The Brainwise Curriculum. http://www.brainwise-plc.org.
9. Lieberman, M. D., Eisenberger, N. I., Crockett, M. J., Tom, S. M., Pfeifer, J. H., & Way, B. M. (2007). Putting feelings into words: Affect labeling disrupts amygdala activity in response to affective stimuli. *Psychological Science, 18,* 421–428.
10. Klein, D. C., Fencil-Morse, E., & Seligman, M. E. (1976). Learning helplessness, depression and the attribution of failure. *Journal of Personality and Social Psychology, 33,* 508–516.
11. Wicks, R. (2007). *The resilient clinician.* London: Oxford University Press.
12. Luders, E., Kurth, F., Mayer, E. A., Toga, A. W., Narr, K. L., & Gaser, C. (2012). The unique brain anatomy of meditation practitioners: Alterations in cortical gyrification. *Frontiers of Human Neuroscience, 6,* 34.
13. Baer, R. A. (2003). Mindfulness training as a clinical intervention: A conceptual and empirical review. *Clinical Psychology: Science and Practice, 10,* 125–143.
14. Shapiro, S., & Carlson, L. (2009). *The art and science of mindfulness.* Washington, DC: American Psychological Association.
15. Schneider, W. J., Cavell, T., & Hughes, J. (2003). A sense of containment: Potential moderator of the relation between parenting practices and children's externalizing behaviors. *Development and Psychopathology, 15,* 95–117.

16. Prochaska, J. O., & DiClemente, C. C. (1983). Stages and processes of self-change of smoking: Toward an integrative model of change. *Journal of Consulting and Clinical Psychology, 51,* 390–395.

17. Shojai, P. (2016). *The urban monk.* New York: Rodale.

18. Halberstadt, A. G., Crisp, V. W., & Eaton, K. L. (1999). Family expressiveness: A retrospective and new directions for research. In P. Philippot, R. S. Feldman, & E. Coats (Eds.), *The social context of nonverbal behavior* (pp. 109–155). New York: Cambridge University Press.

19. Hakim-Larson, J., Parker, A., Lee, C., & Voelker, S. (2006). Measuring parental meta-emotion: Psychometric properties of the emotion-related parenting styles self-test. *Early Education and Development, 17,* 229–251.

20. Duckworth, A., Peterson, C., Matthews, M. D., & Kelly, D. R. (2007). Grit: Perseverance and passion for long-term goals. *Journal of Personality and Social Psychology, 92,* 1087–1101.

21. Creswell, D., Dutcher, J. M., Klein, W. M. P., Harris, P. R., & Levine, J. M. (2013). Self-affirmation improves problem-solving under stress. *PLOS One, 8*(5): e62593. https://doi.org/10.1371/journal.pone.0062593.

22. Barkley, R. A., & Robin, A. L. (2013). *Your defiant teen: 10 steps to resolve conflict and rebuild your relationship* (2nd Ed.). New York: Guilford.

23. Christakis, N. A., & Fowler, J. H. (2011). *Connected: The surprising power of our social networks and how they shape our lives—how your friends' friends' friends affect everything you feel, think and do.* Boston: Back Bay Books.

24. Dweck, C. (2007). *Mindset: The new psychology of success.* New York: Ballantine Books.

25. Neff, K. (2015) *Self-compassion: The proven power of being kind to yourself.* William Morrow Paperbacks.

About the Author

Dr. Mitch Abblett is a clinical psychologist, author, consultant and speaker. As a clinician, his services focus on work with children, teens, parents, families and adults with whom he creates solutions for a range of concerns or desired growth areas. A clinician in the Boston area for over 15 years, he brings a wealth of clinical experience from various settings (hospitals, outpatient clinics, residential facilities and therapeutic schools) to his practice. For 11 years, he served as the Clinical Director of the Manville School at Judge Baker Children's Center in Boston - a Harvard-affiliated therapeutic school program for children and adolescents with emotional, behavioral and learning difficulties. He has also served as the Executive Director of the Institute for Meditation and Psychotherapy.

As a consultant and speaker, Dr. Abblett empowers changes clients through collaborative, tailored interventions. His consultative and training work focuses on mindfulness, compassion and value-driven action and empowering clients to communicate skillfully and authentically. He improves clients' school and work effectiveness, reduces the effects of stress, and increases skills for health self-management and daily productivity. Dr. Abblett's writing includes a mindfulness-based book for clinicians (*The Heat of the Moment: Mindful Management of Difficult Clients*; WW Norton & Co.), *Mindfulness for Teen Depression and Helping Your Angry Teen* (both with New Harbinger), and five decks of mindfulness practice cards such as *Growing Mindful* and *The Self-Compassion Deck* (PESI Publishing). His book, *The Five Hurdles to Happiness-and the Mindful Path to Overcoming Them* was released by Shambhala Publications (August 2018). He also blogs regarding mindfulness applications in family and relationships on Mindful.org.